QUESTIONS OF DIGITAL WORLD

EVERYTHING YOU WANT TO KNOW

SHIVANGA KUMAR GOGOI

This book is dedicated to all my friends, brothers and sisters with love.

Contents

Contents

Preface

In today's age of machines, we use the internet all the time. The internet has become an integral part of our lives. We do different things through the internet. We gain knowledge of various subjects from the Internet. When we do something through the internet or get involved with the internet world, we face various questions in this digital world. Sometimes we get answers to some questions over the internet and do not find answers to some questions. So, we become unable to gain knowledge about those things. Many people personally asked me many such questions. So, I thought of writing a book to answer all the questions of all the people. In this book, I have covered answers to most of the questions. This book is written to answer those questions that arise in our minds. I Hope everyone likes to read this book. The main purpose of writing this book is to provide knowledge of unknown topics of the digital world and inspire you to use them in your daily life by acquiring knowledge about them. I am hopeful that this book will remove all the darkness of the digital world and lead you toward the light. I wish everyone's life shine through digitalization.

Shivanga Kumar Gogoi
21 July 2021
Jorhat, Assam, India

CHAPTER ONE

INTRODUCTION

What is Digital Word?

The term "digital world" refers to the totality of circumstances that characterize the living conditions in the digital age, which will be significantly shaped by a multitude of digital technologies.

The digital world is the world which is connected by digital devices or media. Look around yourself you will only find people indulged in mobile phones, tablets, etc. Almost everything is available online whether it is products or services. This is the digital world that we are creating around ourselves.

Digitalisation gives us the opportunity to express our ideas and opinions. It has given us vocal freedom. Besides that, it has also made lives easier, you don't require to go out for shopping or grocery or cosmetics. You can even learn things online from the comfort of your home.

CHAPTER TWO

AN OPPORTUNITY TO BUILD A DIGITAL WORLD

Recently, the Government of India has banned 59 apps, including TikTok, Share It, Cam Scanner, etc., manufactured and operated by China using Section 69(A) of the Information Technology Act, 2000. The Ministry of Electronics and Information Technology (MeitY) has cited data security and privacy concerns as the basis of the ban.

Since India's digital economy is one of the largest markets in the world and it also has great importance in the global economy. In the era of the digital economy, we can call data the 'currency' of the 21st century. There are many apps that have no means of income, but their only advantage is data collection. This internet-based business model is called surveillance capitalism, where all social media apps and other such platform users who collect money from users use their respective data and get income from it.

Chinese apps banned in India are an example of surveillance capitalism.

The ban on Chinese equipment imposed by India has certainly negatively affected the credibility of Chinese companies in the global market. This has come as an opportunity for India. India has to move towards digitalization while working on a long-term strategy. Experts believe that the Indian digital economy can become the leader of the digital world.

Meaning of the digital economy

- The form of the economic system in which most of the money is transacted through credit cards, debit cards, net banking, mobile payments and other digital means is called the digital economy.
- Digital services have become important for the 21st-century economy. When more traditional modes of commercial transactions were disrupted in the event of national or global emergencies, digital services have succeeded in filling such gaps that have been created.
- Digital services enable access to and distribution of a wide variety of products in many areas, from health services and retail delivery to financial services.

Components of the Digital Economy

- In view of the changing scenario in the country, the digital economy can be divided into three main components:

- The Government of India's Digital India programme has promoted financial inclusion as well as the use of digital infrastructure. The plan to provide countrywide access to digital infrastructure, including high-speed WiFi, has boosted the digital economy in India.
- The second phase of the digital economy is the growth of electronic and mobile commerce in India. The technologically savvy young generation considers online purchases as the simplest means of purchasing goods. This has led to the expansion of e-commerce and m-commerce in the country.
- The utility of data at every level in the digital economy is increasing. Our economy is going through a phase of understanding and analyzing such data. In view of this, the Government of India has launched its own open data portal where data is available for analysis.
- Given the ever-increasing volume of data and the strategic importance, the Government is assisting in providing training and research in the field of data analytics for the digital economy.

What is Big Data?

- Big data is a phrase that is used for a very large amount of structured and unstructured data, which is so large that it is extremely difficult to process it using traditional databases and software techniques.
- Big Data is used in industries by analyzing the customer's behaviour through data obtained from social

media by the use of a highly advanced variety of computing and algorithms and by estimating his or her interest-distaste.

India, the hub of digital innovation

- Digital India is becoming a medium of digital empowerment by creating the necessary digital infrastructure to provide services in the country digitally. In a world where geographical distances are no longer a barrier to building a better future, India has emerged as a powerful hub of digital innovation in every field.
- With over one lakh villages connected with optical fibre, 121 crore mobile phones, about 122 crores Aadhaar and 50 crore internet service users, India is now the country with the largest population in the world associated with ease with technology.
- The high-speed internet 5G service in India is likely to be launched in the year 2020. The use of 5G technology will not be limited to browsing on mobiles and laptops, it will also be able to make new technological developments in health, agriculture and industry-related areas. Due to the fast internet speed and low latency, it will also prove to be useful in serverless applications, remote control surgery, and connected smart cities.
- Artificial intelligence is going to play an important role in the field of economic development and social progress and is also doing so. India's goal is to develop man-centric artificial intelligence, which can benefit

humanity in an inclusive manner. Finding solutions to difficult problems and being among the world's leading countries in the field of Artificial Intelligence is one of India's major goals.

- At present, the tech-efficient economy is playing a major role in determining the country's foreign policy. Cyber-secure India's 5G internet technology will prove to be an important factor in determining its relationship with developing countries.

Problems in India's digitalization

- **Lack of necessary infrastructure:** According to a report by ASSOCHAM and Daylight, there are many challenges in ensuring the successful implementation of the ambitious digital ecosystem due to ambiguity and structural difficulties in policies. Apart from this, frequent breakdown of network connectivity or server failure also creates difficulty.
- **Digital Divide:** For the development of digital ecology, there is a need to eliminate the digital divide by providing adequate connectivity even in remote villages. There are still more than 50,000 villages in the country where mobile connectivity is not available.
- **Cyber security issue:** India's existing Information Technology Law is not very effective in preventing cyber crimes. Apart from the cloning of ATM cards, complaints of bank accounts being hacked, data and confidential information reaching the hackers are being reported from time to time. In such a situation, unless stringent provisions are included in the law regarding

cyber crimes, the process of digitalization will not get the speed that is required.

- **Increase in inequalities:** Success in the digital provision of services is dependent on many underlying factors, including digital literacy, education, and access to stable and fast telecommunication services. The massive digitalization of services without addressing these issues could result in an increase in existing inequalities.
- **The challenge of data protection:** In the 21st century, data is as important as currency. Due to India's huge population, many international companies (Google, Amazon etc.) are trying to make their way here. Therefore, it is necessary to address the issues related to data sovereignty, data localisation and internet governance etc.

Government's efforts toward digitalization

National Digital Literacy Mission

- The National Digital Literacy Mission has been launched with the objective of making at least one person digitally literate in every household in India by the year 2020.
- The aim of this project is to help technically illiterate adults find their place in a rapidly digitalizing world.

National Digital Communications Policy-2018

- Providing universal broadband connectivity to every citizen at a speed of 50 Mbps.
- Providing connectivity of 1 Gbps by 2020 and 10 Gbps by 2022 to all Gram Panchayats.
- Setting up a National Digital Grid by creating a National Fibre Authority.
- Ensure connectivity to areas which have not yet been covered.
- Attracting investment of $100 billion for the digital communications sector.

National Cyber Security Policy, 2013

- The 'National Cyber Security Policy, 2013' was released by the government under which the 'National Critical Information Infrastructure Protection Centre (NCIIPC) was set up to protect highly sensitive information.'
- India is coordinating with countries like the US, UK and Israel to adopt the best practices in terms of information sharing and cyber security.

The Personal Data Protection Bill, 2019

- The Government of India had also introduced the Personal Data Protection Bill, 2019 in the Lok Sabha during the winter session.

- The Bill has been referred to the Joint Parliamentary Committee for wider consideration where the points included in the Bill will be discussed extensively.
- The Personal Data Protection Law is a comprehensive law that seeks to give individuals more control over how their personal data is collected, stored, and used.

E-Commerce Policy:

- In the field of e-commerce, problems such as consumer protection, data privacy and providing equal opportunities to stakeholders have been coming to the fore. The National E-commerce Policy formulates a strategy with the aim of providing appropriate solutions to these problems.
- The policy also takes into account the interests of domestic manufacturers and micro, small and medium enterprises, as well as making the online marketplace an equal zone for them.

The road ahead

- **Repeal of obsolete laws:** India's digital applications are governed by obsolete laws, which have become unsuitable in the context of the current digital landscape.

- **The Information Technology Act, 2000** was designed for the business process outsourcing ecosystem and not for modern digital applications or platforms.
- Similarly, the **Copyright Act**, which provides incentives and protections for most of the content at the heart of the digital economy, was last amended in 2012.
- Thus, strong willpower is needed to amend the major laws and adapt them to the digital environment.

Taking advantage of the available opportunity

- The government will have to provide incentives to young entrepreneurs in the development of Indian equipment in place of the banned Chinese equipment.
- For speedy construction of any technical project, it is necessary to have single window clearance, availability of funds and no objection certificate facility. The Government should act swiftly in this direction.
- The recent ban on Chinese equipment is a good opportunity for Indian entrepreneurs to fill the void that has arisen in the market.
- With the help of technically skilled Indian professionals, India can soon become a hub of digital innovation in the world.

CHAPTER THREE

WHAT IS HTTP?

Today, the internet is used by almost everyone. Whenever you open a browser to search for something through the Internet, you will see some words, HTTP and HTTPS in the address bar of the browser. Looking at these words, the question must have been raised in your mind what is HTTP or what is HTTPS?

You may have seen that "not secure" with HTTP and "green lock" symbol and "secure" with HTTPS are written, we will talk about why HTTPS is secure. Here you also get confused by seeing why the addresses of different websites are not in different formats. To get the answers to all these questions, let's get started and know what HTTP is.

What is HTTP?

HTTP is a type of Internet protocol whose full name is **Hypertext Transfer Protocol**. It is a protocol that accesses data on the World Wide Web. It is a computer communication protocol used for communication on the web around the world. The protocol is a set of rules that operate the client/server between your web browser and the web page. As the name suggests, this HTTP is a text transfer protocol, so we can see everything we see on any website only through HTTP.

As I mentioned earlier, HTTP is written before the address of a website (e.g. http://www.abc.com). When there is any kind of data such as text, audio, video, image, etc. between a browser and a server, they have to follow certain rules and these rules are determined by the HTTP protocol. Through the protocol, it is determined what the format and transmission of the data to be transferred will be and what the response of the browser and server will be to different commands.

How does HTTP work?

As I've already mentioned, HTTP is a communication protocol. It creates communication between the client and the server. When a client requests a website server, HTTP accepts that request and establishes communication between the client and the server through TCP. Then HTTP sends the request to the server, all the files are stored on the server. From here, HTTP draws the requested information and transmits it to the client.

HTTP Error Code

The HTTP error code is a response sent by the client to the server's request. For example, when your client (your web browser) tries to connect to the server. These responses include redirects, server errors, client errors, etc. HTTP error codes are not related to web pages, instead, they are responses received from the server on how to process the request.

The 7 Most Common HTTP Error Codes

1. 401 Unauthorized

401 is the first error code on our list. The 401 error indicates that the server has received an unauthorized request. When this error occurs, the system displays a message that states that the page cannot be loaded because of invalid credentials for various reasons.

2. 404 not found

404 is a common HTTP error code on the internet. This HTTP response will occur when the page the user is looking for is not found on the server. There may be many reasons behind the 404 error. Maybe because the webmaster didn't create the page or the URL you entered is incorrect (because it's a client error).

3. 500 internal server error

A 500 internal server error is a common error, it occurs when a problem occurs in your server. There are many different reasons for this, including WordPress plugins, PHP, databases, etc.

4. 502 Bad Gateway

Unlike other HTTP error codes, 502 is different. When one server on the Internet receives an invalid response from another server, a bad gateway error occurs. When the server takes longer than expected to complete the request, the 502 HTTP status code will appear on the screen.

5. 301 Moved Permanently

HTTP 301 is an error of moving a specific web page permanently to another URL. This by itself is not an error, but it conveys important information. This can be at the page level where you can point to another similar post (or even homepage) or domain at that page level. In simple words, any webpage on another URL is called Permanently Redirect 301 Redirect.

6. Discovery 302

It is similar to HTTPttp status code 301 but is used for temporary redirection. This response tells Google that the page has been temporarily redirected and will return to the original URL at some point. If done correctly, it will redirect the user to another URL in a few seconds.

7. 410 went

This is similar to the 410 Gone error 404 error. Think of it as permanently 404. When webmasters decide to permanently delete a post or page or restore it to another site, they can use this code.

410 Feedback informs Google that the requested resource has been permanently removed from the Internet and will not reappear. This way, you can easily crawl or index web pages from Google.

Why isn't HTTP secure?

If you're looking at the "Not Secure" warning, it's because the web page or website you're visiting isn't providing a secure connection. If you are using these websites for any transaction etc. then you should avoid these websites. Login here, providing personal information or giving payment information should be avoided. Browsing such unsecured sites can put you at risk. No secure warning indicates a lack of security for the connection to that page. It is alerting you that the information sent and received with that page is unsafe. This could potentially be stolen, read, or modified by attackers, hackers, and entities through access to internet infrastructures, such as **Internet Service Providers (ISPs)** and governments.

What is HTTPS?

HTTPS stands for **HyperText Transfer Protocol Secure**. This is the Secured version of HTTP. The HTTPS protocol uses **SSL (Secured Socket Layer)** and **TLS (Transport Layer Security)** protocols for encrypted transmission and identity authentication. It mainly uses digital certificates, encryption algorithms, asymmetric keys, and other technologies to complete internet data transmission security to obtain internet transmission security. It communicates data in an encrypted form, unlike HTTP. HTTPS is only related to the client and the server, between which the data cannot be read by any other person. To get HTTPS, both the client and the server have to verify their identity to prove whether the identity of the person who is getting the communication is real or not. HTTPS is used in security-sensitive communication on the World Wide Web such as transactions, and payments. There are three main goals:

- **Data confidentiality:** To ensure that the data will not be viewed by any third party during transmission. Like the delivery of a package by a courier, all packages are packed, and others can't know what's inside.
- **Data integrity:** Periodically check if the data has been tampered with by a third party.
- **Data Authentication:** Here, clients and servers have to do their identity verification. Just like when we mail a package, although it is a packaged package that has not been replaced, it should be ensured that the package will not be sent in the wrong place, and data authentication is used to make sure that it is sent to the right place.

How does HTTPS work?

HTTPS also works in the same way as HTTP, the only difference here is that through HTTPS all the data is encrypted and transferred from the server to the client. It works on the concept of cryptography. Cryptography is an encrypting method by which plain text is converted into an unreadable format. Due to this, apart from the authorized user, no hackers, etc., can read the information from the third party.

What's the difference between HTTP and HTTPS?

- The main differences between HTTPS and HTTP are as follows:
- The full form of HTTP is a hypertext transfer protocol. The full form of HTTPS is Hypertext Transfer Protocol

Secure.

- Http URLs start with http:// while https URLs start with https://.
- HTTPS acts on an SSL certificate that requires a certification authority to apply. HTTP does not require a certificate.
- HTTP is a hypertext transmission protocol, where information is transferred to plain text, and HTTPS is a secure SSL encrypted transmission protocol.
- HTTP and HTTPS use completely different connection methods and use different ports. It uses HTTP 80 ports and HTTPS 443 ports.
- The HTTP connection is very simple and stateless; The HTTPS protocol is a network protocol designed for transmission and identity authentication encrypted by the SSL+ HTTP protocol, which is more secure than the HTTP protocol.

Friends, here I told you what is HTTP, and how HTTP work. What's the difference between HTTPS and HTTP? What are HTTP error codes?

CHAPTER FOUR

WHAT IS UPI?

UPI stands for Unified Payments Interface, the latest means of making internet-based payment payments. To use UPI, you need a bank account, its associated mobile number and a mobile app. If your smartphone has a UPI app then you can easily transfer money.

Various modes of payment prevalent before UPI

Since ancient times, the currency has been transacted for trade exchange. Over time, there has been a change in the form of currency. Precious metal coins like cowries, leather coins, gold and silver, paper notes, etc., have been used at different times. As technology evolved, so did the methods of payment. The time of cheques, demand drafts, pay orders, money orders, etc., also came and went. In today's time, the emergence of the internet has provided new dimensions like ATM, NEFT, RTGS, SWIFT, IMPS, BHIM and UPI for payment. All these mediums have reduced cashless transactions significantly, and by tapping a few clicks and mobile screens, we can transfer or receive money in a pinch. Ever since the use of UPI has increased, some new types of fraud have also started happening, we will also read how can you keep yourself safe from online frauds.

What is UPI?

In 2008, the Reserve Bank of India and other large banks formed an institution called the National Payments Corporation of India (NPCI). The main objective of this non-profit organization is to facilitate the transaction of money in the economy of the country. In this episode, NPCI launched UPI in 2016. Your bank's UPI app allows you to register a virtual payment address (VPA). Using this you can provide an ad-hoc payment. The format of the VPA is similar to that of an email address, for example, something like this:

VPA Example: username@bankid

You can make the payment immediately by entering the VAPA ID of any beneficiary on your UPI app. The facility works 24 hours a day and seven days. You can make money transactions with it on Sundays and other holidays.

CHAPTER FIVE

What is Cache Memory?

I will tell you what is cache memory and how much it is. Many of us are always connected to mobiles and computers. But many of us don't know what cache memory is. For this reason, we will learn in detail about cache memory. What is cache memory and how many types of types does it usually be? What is cache? How many types of cache memory are there?

In our computers, we usually know two types of memory. One is the primary memory called ROM (hard disk), and the other is temporary memory called RAM. But apart from these two, there is another type of memory that we have included in all these types of devices and that is cache memory. But many of us don't know what cache memory is and how it works on our devices. So let's know.

What is cache memory?

Cache Memory is a chip-based computer device that acts as a temporary storage area to hold the necessary data in the CPU. This temporary storage device called cache is located very close to the processor. Cache memory is often referred to as **CPU (Central Processing Unit)** memory because it is usually located directly inside the CPU chip. It is connected to a separate bus (computer bus) with the CPU in a computer. Since it is very close to the processor, it is very small in size and its storage space is also very small. Cache memory is more expensive than primary memory. Cache memory is usually 10 to 100 times faster than RAM, which can deliver output in just a few nanoseconds. The hardware used in the cache memory is called "**High-Speed Static Random Access Memory (SRAM)**".

As I mentioned earlier cache memory is very low in a computer or mobile, which means that where your hard disk can be up to several hundred GB, this cache memory has two to three MB.

How does cache memory work?

The working of cache memory is quite simple. When we use it, cache memory stores our data or information. It reprocesses it back in the shortest and fastest time it needs.

In short, any of our data without cache memory will be output by a computer or mobile processor, but that data will reach us through the processor through the signal input device, then it will be active through signal RAM and delivered to the processor, then our work will be completed.

Cache memory stores various information that we input first, so whenever we want to revisit or process that information, it starts to be processed directly from the cache to the processor rather than the ram. Having cache memory allows us to run many things on our computer or mobile at the same time.

How many types of cache memory are there?

So far we've learned what cache memory is and how it works. But there are many types of cache memory. Now let's see what form this cache memory can generally be divided into –

Browser Cache:

Most browsers store a variety of website data in cache memory. This means that when we visit a website, the various information of those websites is stored in the cache memory. Because the next time we enter the same website, the processor can restore things in front of us very fast. And all CSS or java files of that website are stored in cache memory. The cache memory stores all these data to make the CPU work. Generally, any website is created with Java, and CSS files, all of these files contain some files that makeup cookies. And these cookies usually contain different topics of any website. All of this information is stored in the web browser's cache memory, either be it an image, a CSS file, or a variety of JavaScript types of JavaScript. For this reason, when we need those websites a second time, it is possible to display them from cache memory without processing. This reduces the stress on other memory. Here's another thing to note that I mentioned earlier cache memory is usually added to two to three MB, but sometimes the cache data of an application we look at from 400 to 500 MB, you will think how this is possible. Although the cache memory is very low, it can store any data in its RAM and hard disk memory. So all the storage we see is usually storage taken from RAM and ROM.

Memory Cache;

When we start an application or project, part of that project is stored in our system memory or RAM. As a result, since RAM is a fast-paced memory, it is not necessary to process that data from a hard disk or ROM, it is processed from a memory cache. This process is especially seen in the case of some large-sized applications. For example, in the case of a video editing app, when we edit a video, even if we remove a short clip from the editor, we can easily bring it back. This means that if it is removed from the editor, it is stored in cache memory, so there is no need to re-add the clip from the hard disk.

Disk Cache:

For most hard drives and solid state drives or SSDs, we see a certain amount of cache memory. Usually, a computer processor has two to three MB or more cache memory. But this cache memory on the hard drive or SSD is given as a fixed amount. For example, in the case of a 1TB hard disk, 32 MB of cache memory is provided. This means that a certain amount of cache memory is given in the various disk storages of the computer or mobile so that it can be combined with the processor or CPU's cache and the cache of these disks can be done at a faster speed than any work. Suppose when we open a folder on the computer, if that folder contains a thousand types of information, it gradually starts opening up in front of us. After seeing that information, we close that folder. This does not mean that the process data is deleted as soon as the folder is closed. They are stored in the memory of the disk cache. If we need to reopen that folder, then as soon as we open it, all the data inside it will open automatically. This means that its process disk cache is stored in memory, so it opens a second time without taking much time.

Processor Cache:

Processor Cache Memory The function of cache memory is to improve CPU speed and performance, usually divided into "levels" based on the accessibility of the CPU. Cache memory is divided into different levels, which are L1, L2 and L3.

L1 Cache: The L1 cache is also called the primary cache. It is very fast but relatively small (size 2KB to 64KB). It is usually located in the processor chip.

L2 Cache: L2 Cache is also known as Secondary Cache. Its capacity is higher than that of the L1 Cache (256KB to 512KB). The L2 cache stays on the CPU but sometimes it can also be on a different chip, in which case it is connected to the CPU by a dedicated system bus. If the CPU could not find instruction in the L1 cache, it searches in the L2 cache.

L3 Cache: The L3 Cache has been developed to improve the performance of the L2 Cache. The L3 cache has a capacity greater than L1 and L2 (its size can range from 1MB to 8MB) but it is slower than other caches. However, the speed of the L3 is twice that of the DRAM. In CPUs with multiple cores, it is usually seen that there is a separate dedicated L1 and L2 cache for each core but only one L3 cache.

Cache memory is a very important component that is required for all types of memory storage connected to the computer. If our memory will not be connected to the processor, it will take more time for the computer to process any data. That's why we need a lot of this cached memory on mobile or computers and even laptops. However, it should be kept in mind that cache memory alone cannot be fast. To make the device fast, there is a combination of several processes, which require cache memory.

CHAPTER SIX

WHAT IS YOUTUBE?

You must have seen a lot of videos on YouTube, but do you know what YouTube is, how to use it and how to earn from it? If not, it doesn't matter, because, in this chapter, I will tell you about all this in detail (full information about YouTube). There is hardly a person who uses a smartphone and has not seen videos on YouTube, but still many people do not have information about YouTube.

What is YouTube?

YouTube is a video-watching website in the US, in which you can watch the videos of others as well as upload your videos. YouTube lets its registered members upload videos, watch, share, add favourite videos, report, comment, and subscribe to other members' channels. But people use it the most to watch videos. It is full of entertainment, comedy, movies, clips, trailers, etc. YouTube's goal is to bring everyone's voice to the world and make them familiar with the world. Learn about our brand, community, career, etc.

Who created YouTube?

It was created in February 2005 by three former PayPal employees, Chad Hurley, Steve Chan and Javed Karim, and was purchased by Google in November 2006 for US$1.65 billion. Now its owner is Google E and it is counted among google's services. It is the world's largest video-sharing platform. Millions of videos have been uploaded on it.

History of YouTube

- Three former PayPal employees, Chad Hurley, Steve Chan, and Javed Karim, created the YouTube website in 2005. In November 2006, Google bought it for $1.65 billion.
- In October 2008, Google announced that it had signed an agreement for $1.45 billion to acquire a company and that it had completed the agreement on November 13, 2008, after Google completed the agreement with YouTube on November 14, 2007.
- The first video on YouTube was uploaded by co-founder Javed Karim, titled Me at the Zoo. The video showed the San Diego Zoo.
- The video was uploaded on April 23, 2005, and can still be viewed on YouTube.

How did YouTube start?

According to one story, Hurley and Chan had difficulty sharing videos drawn at a dinner party at Chen's apartment in San Francisco during the early months of 2005. It is believed that this is what led to the birth of the idea of YouTube. But Karim did not join the party and has categorically denied that the party was held, but he was not there. Karim has described not getting video clips of the 2004 Indian Ocean tsunami online as an "inspiration for YouTube". This made him think that a platform should be created that had videos from all over the world and could be seen if needed.

The Social Impact of YouTube

Before the launch of YouTube in 2005, there were very few or no equivalent methods available for online video posts for common computer users. YouTube has made this process easier. Now you can post any video from your computer or mobile by using its easy interface. Which millions of people can see in a few minutes. YouTube has made video sharing with diverse topics the most important part of the Internet culture. Today it has become so popular that people can't live without watching videos on YouTube. Now it has become the favourite platform for people to watch entertainment, news, movies, etc.

How to use YouTube?

YouTube is very easy to use, any user can use it on their mobile phone, computer, or laptop through its website or its app. Its website has the URL YouTube.com and you can also use its apps for Android, Windows, iOS, Mac, iPad, etc.

You can use YouTube in 2 ways.

- To watch videos
- To share videos

Now let's know in a little detail about it, what happens by watching and uploading videos on YouTube.

How to watch videos on YouTube and why?

There can be many reasons to watch videos on YouTube. Everyone wants to watch videos on YouTube for different reasons. As if,

- To get information.
- For fun
- To watch the news
- To watch movies or trailers of movies
- New songs, songs to see
- And for many other reasons.

People use YouTube more for entertainment. Apart from this, it is used to obtain information.

For example, if you are a student, then you can watch videos related to your studies and exam-related information, or if you need any help, then you can watch the video of it.

How to upload videos to YouTube and why?

It's very easy to share videos on YouTube. For this, you just have to create a YouTube channel by logging in to YouTube from your Google Gmail ID. After that, you can start uploading videos on YouTube. Now the question is why you should upload videos on YouTube.

At the same time, you might be wondering why do people upload videos on YouTube. So let me tell you that it earns those people. You can also earn money by uploading videos on YouTube.

How do you earn from YouTube?

To earn money from YouTube, you have to create a channel on it. After the channel is created, you can create and upload videos on your channel. Remember, you have to make a video by yourself and upload it.

After that, when the views on your videos start coming, then you can start making money by monetizing your YouTube channel.

So this was the information about what YouTube is and how to use it. At the same time, we also learned about making money from YouTube. If you want, you can earn lakhs of rupees by working on YouTube. A lot of YouTubers are also earning.

CHAPTER SEVEN

How to Become a Successful YouTuber?

Do you know who YouTubers are? Today, "YouTube" has become a huge video search engine. Today, anyone who has a smartphone must use YouTube. YouTube is a video-based app owned by Google.

Many watch YouTube just for fun but many want to make YouTube a source of their earnings. They do a lot of research on the internet on the subject of how to upload videos on YouTube?, and how to make money from YouTube. Today, YouTube is the source of earnings for someone and education for someone. So you can also earn money from it by helping other people by uploading videos on YouTube.

People who make videos on YouTube or who are fond of video editing or anything else and pass on their skills to other people through YouTube are called YouTubers in simple language. And the work they do is called YouTubing or vlogging. But not everyone is a successful YouTuber posting videos on YouTube. So the thing to pay attention to is how to become a successful YouTuber. Today, I am going to explain in detail how to become a successful YouTuber. What things do you need to keep in mind to become a successful youth? Or what mistakes you should avoid, we will discuss all this in this chapter. So let's get started.

Who is called a YouTuber?

If you want to start or do something online you will often hear two words, the first blogger and the second YouTuber, but do you understand the true meaning of Blogger and YouTuber? You can understand this in simple language, the person who works on a website or blog, or runs a blog is called a blogger, and a person who makes a video on a YouTube channel or runs a YouTube channel is called a YouTuber.

Many people who have a website or blog create a YouTube channel to promote their blog and promote their blog through it. In this way, if their YouTube channel becomes popular, then they are called bloggers as well as YouTubers.

On the other hand, the person who has a YouTube channel also creates a website to provide content in writing to their subscribers and promote their YouTube videos online. After the website becomes popular, they are popularized as YouTubers as well as bloggers. So now you must have understood what is the difference between a blogger and a YouTuber and how they both work.

However, the work of a blogger or YouTuber is something in which they live their lives. They don't work under anyone. They don't have a boss. So in this way, they work when they are in mind without any worries and at the same time earn good money. They can work on a blog or YouTube channel by opening an office from anywhere or sitting at home. And sitting at home, people can share knowledge, tips, opinions, experiences, etc. online.

How many types of YouTubers are there?

Today you will find a variety of channels on YouTube that provide different types of information. Many YouTubers give information related to technology, many provide information related to gaming, entertainment, astrology, health and fitness, recipe, education, legal, etc. There are a lot of categories to create channels on YouTube. You can create a channel related to the topic you are interested in, but keep in mind that you post things that people search about. Here's something special about YouTubers.

Tech YouTuber: This is a YouTube celebrity who posts videos related to technology on his channel. On this type of channel, information about the technical news, gadgets, etc. happening all over the world is given. Some of the youtube channels associated with technology in India are Technical Guruji, Trakin Tech, Sidtalk, Tech Burner, etc.

Entertainment Youtuber: It is YouTube celebrities who rule people's hearts by entertaining them. They publish such video content on their channels that can make people laugh and entertain them. Some of the popular entertainment channels on YouTube are Amit Bhadana, BB ki Vines and Carryminati.

Vlogger: These are YouTubers that go for a walk in different places and make a video of the scenes there and upload it on YouTube and present them in front of people. A lot of people like to see such a scene. Because the fun of enjoying the beautiful nature scene is something different.

Some of the famous Indian YouTube channels associated with Vlogging are Web Beast, Mumbiker Nikhil and Gaurav Zone, Gaurav Chaudhari etc.

Gaming YouTubers: These are YouTubers who love to play games. They upload YouTube videos related to gaming on their channel. They also stream live videos while playing games for people. Some of the famous Indian Gaming YouTube channels are Carryislive, Dynamo Gaming, Scout and Mortal.

Which topic to choose to create a YouTube channel?

Although you can create a YouTube channel on any topic according to your skills, youTube channels based on the following topics are currently making a lot of money.

Technology – Today, videos related to technology are being posted everywhere on YouTube. This is because technology is one of the most popular topics in the world today. So if you make videos about this, a lot of people will watch your video and earn a lot more. But there is little competitiveness in this subject, but if you work hard, then success will be achieved. And once you have success, you will become a successful YouTuber.

App Review Channel – Nowadays Android apps are used a lot. You and I all have fun installing new apps on mobile. But, we don't know about all the apps and so people on the internet come to know about the new and interesting apps. So, you can go to the Google Play Store, learn about the best apps, create videos associated with them and upload them to your channel.

Mobile Phone Review – In today's time, many people are making money from YouTube. And if you want, you can also create videos about mobiles by creating a new mobile review channel on your channel. The better you tell about mobile, the more people will like your video. And that way people will also subscribe to the channel to get your new videos because a lot of people like to get information about the new smartphone.

Tutorial Video Channel – Nowadays everyone is making their channel successful by uploading some tutorial videos on their channel. This is because tutorial videos are the most popular on the internet and so people keep searching for different types of tutorials on YouTube. Tutorial videos can be anything that explains something to you. I mean, you can make videos about how to do anything, how to make it, how to start something and put it on your channel.

Food Channel – If you like to cook new food, you can find success by making your food recipe video on YouTube. You can run your food video channel by making a video of making new dishes by yourself and showing you how to make the food.

Blogging Tips – Nowadays people search for a lot of information on the internet to learn about blogging. So, if you can create and upload tutorial videos related to blogging and WordPress, that channel will be very popular.

Online Earning Tips – Nowadays everyone is looking for new ways to earn money online from home. So, you can share the latest earning tips and tutorials on the internet via video. People like this kind of video a lot.

Gaming Channel – A lot of people like to play games today. Today, many people take smartphones to games. You can play games on your mobile or computer, record them and upload gameplay videos to your channel. Nowadays, this type of gaming channel is gaining popularity very fast.

Above I have given you some ideas to create YouTube channels which are very popular nowadays and people are earning lakhs of rupees by uploading videos on these channels. So, you can also create channels on these topics if you want.

How to become a successful YouTuber? (Tips to Become a Successful YouTuber)

It has become very difficult to work in any field today. There is a lot of competition in every field today. Today it has become very difficult to achieve success in any field. But keep in mind, that it is difficult but not impossible to achieve success in any field. All you have to do is use some method and make a little change in the way you do it.

A successful YouTuber means that you have a lot of subscribers on your YouTube channel. Get more likes, comments and replies. Today there are a lot of YouTubers who are uploading videos to YouTube and they are making so much money online from their YouTube channel that they don't need to do anything else.

In addition, many YouTubers are so successful that they are running their YouTube channel as a business. To become a successful YouTuber, you must work by setting a goal. Once your YouTube channel is on the road to success, it can make you an owner of millions of dollars.

Creating a successful YouTube channel simply needs to work with your mind. If you have the interest, enthusiasm, and desire to succeed at work, you can be a successful and talented YouTuber. Follow the tips given below to become a successful YouTuber.

- Make videos about popular and work topics.

- Make interesting and informative videos.
- Pay attention to YouTube's SEO.
- Create quality and creative videos.
- Be consistent – upload videos regularly.

Things you need to become a YouTuber

It's not enough to have just one YouTube channel to become a YouTuber. Apart from this, you need some special skills and a little knowledge. Here a skill is required that you can show in front of other people and it should be accompanied by knowledge so that you can edit the video. However, you can also hire a video editor by paying some money. If you work with a few days of patience, then you will one day become a successful YouTuber.

To achieve success on YouTube, you must have your unique content. Because any user expects new and interesting content from you. Unless the content is strong, the ranking of your channel cannot remain stable. And to create a quality video you need a few things that are following.

Mike - Mike is very important to make YouTube videos If you make a YouTube video without a mic, then your audio will not be recorded properly. For YouTube videos, you have to go to a quiet environment and record the audio using a good mic. You need to explain to the user that it is well visible and heard, and if your voice is not cleared then your viewer will have trouble.

Camera: It is very important to have a great camera to make YouTube videos. Nowadays people think that you record a video from the mobile and put it on YouTube, but it will be better if you buy a good camera separately.

Although nowadays mobile is also getting the best camera, you can also use mobile for it if you want.

Video Editing Software: If you record the video, then you need video editing software to give it a professional look. Video editing software is very important to delete some parts of the video or to add animation to the video. On the internet, you will find a lot of video editing software for PC and mobile. Kinemaster and Filmora are very popular among the best video editing software on PCs.

Patience: Patience is required to do any task and especially in any online business. Because no one's own business is such that earning starts as soon as you start. Many YouTubers get frustrated when they don't get views when they put 1 to 2 videos and stop posting videos. So don't be disappointed, one day your video will rank. Don't stop working hard. Because millions of videos are uploaded on YouTube daily, it will take a while for your video to rank.

Mobile/ Laptop: It is necessary to have a mobile or laptop to upload videos and edit videos on YouTube. You can also do video recording or editing from mobile, but I would recommend you use a laptop or desktop if you want to stay a YouTuber for a long time or become a professional YouTuber.

Qualification for Becoming a YouTuber

To become a YouTuber you do not have to take any course nor do you need any degree for it. For this, you just need to have a little bit of information about the topic that your YouTube channel is associated with. You can do research on the internet for that topic or watch a YouTube video related to your topic. All you have to do is focus on your skill development. All you have to keep in mind is that you should know enough about the topic you are going to tell people about because your video will be seen by many people and you can be asked many questions related to that video. If you are streaming live videos on YouTube, then at this time you will be asked a question through live chat. You may think that if you do not give the right answer, then what will be the effect on the user? So do some research before making a video.

Apart from this, you should upload the video to YouTube, optimize it for the search engine or publish it. For this, you should also come with video editing. If you do not know video editing, then you can also do online or offline courses for it or you can hire another video editor and get the video editing done by paying some money.

Ways to Make Money from YouTube

After creating a YouTube channel, if you have more than 1000 subscribers, then you can earn a little bit. Later, your earnings continue to grow depending on the work. Here are all the means you can make money through YouTube.

Google AdSense: You can easily earn income by showing Google Adsense ads in your videos. It's the easiest, most popular, and most profitable way. For this, you need to apply for Google AdSense. You can apply for Google AdSense when 1000 subscribers and 4000 hours of watch time on your channel are complete. You can click on this link to read how to increase YouTube's watch time.

First of all, you have to turn on the Monetization option of the YouTube channel, and then connect it to Google AdSense. After this, the ads will be shown after your video is played. The more ads are shown, the more you'll be able to earn. CPC and CTR are very important here. If you put a good quality video, then it will get good views, along with this, the search engine optimization of the video is also necessary. When your earnings are 100 USD, they will then be remitted to your bank account.

Sponsorship: Sponsorship is another way to make money from YouTube. You can earn lakhs of rupees from sponsorship, but for that, you have to have a big YouTube channel. Sponsorship requires a channel that has become a brand. You recommend someone on such a channel to your customers for the product of a particular company. For this, the company gives you money.

Affiliate Marketing: Affiliate marketing is a killer way to make money from YouTube. Here you can promote products of other companies through your channel/ channel. You have to do marketing. If someone buys the product you promote, you will get a good commission from the company for that sale. It's currently the best business model.

Apart from these three ways, you can also earn money by promoting your services and products.

And, if you have a YouTube channel which has more subscribers and you are not working on it or do not want to do so, then you can also earn good money by selling that channel.

CHAPTER EIGHT

How to increase YouTube Watch Time?

Do you want to know how to increase YouTube's watch time? How to keep users connected to your YouTube channel for a longer period?

The number of people posting videos on YouTube is increasing day by day. Today, many video creators resort to YouTube to present their skills to people. So Google is also always bringing some updates so that creators focus more on creating videos and quality content is posted on YouTube. Because today there is a lot of competition on YouTube, due to which people have to work very hard to rank their videos despite putting quality content. If the terms and conditions of YouTube are not changed from time to time, then you may have a huge crowd of creators on YouTube whose content has no substance. And if such creators come, it will be more difficult for YouTubers who create good content to rank their videos.

However, even today, many creators do not make a video by themselves and make a little change in someone else's video and put it on their channel. But they don't make money from YouTube. Because Google has made it clear in an update that you need to have 4000 hours of watch time and 1000 subscribers to show ads in your video. Users like attractive and unique videos. They are always looking for new content. If you want to show them old content, why would they watch it when there is already a lot of original and high-quality content on YouTube?

Today in this chapter, I am going to tell you how to increase your watch time on YouTube. Today, you will learn in detail about the important way to increase the watch time on YouTube. So let's get started.

How to Increase YouTube Watch Time?

YouTube Watch Time is the total time that users spend watching a video uploaded to your channel. You can view your channel's total watch time using YouTube Analytics.

Friends, to earn money from YouTube i.e. for the monetization of YouTube, you have to take the approval of Google AdSense so that ads are shown with video and you are earned through Google Adsense. But for the approval of Google Adsense on YouTube, you need to have 4000 hours of watch time, that is, the video you uploaded should be viewed by the users for 4000 hours, only then you will get the approval of Google AdSense. Seeing this, many YouTubers get scared and start thinking about how to increase their YouTube Watch time. So here are some important tips for this so that you can increase your YouTube Watch time.

1. Create videos about popular and work topics

Many YouTubers start making videos according to their interest. Many people give them such advice that you should make a video on the same topic that you are interested in. But, I say, make videos based on people's interests. Make videos that are in high demand, videos that people search for a lot on YouTube.

Because, if you make a video of your interest, people may not be searching on the internet for that video. Because the user and your thinking will be very different. So you will keep making videos but you will not get views on them. And if the views don't come, how will the watch time increase? Therefore, you have to look for a topic that is very popular among people, or a topic that is very much searched for on YouTube.

You need to do keyword research before creating a video. You can use any online tool to do keyword research for YouTube so that you know which keywords you want to use and how often the keyword you are using is searched.

2. Create attractive content

The first thing you have to pay attention to increase YouTube Watch time is what is the user's demand. You don't create useless content. You should first think about what the user likes. In the first 15 seconds of the video, you have to tell about the video or show something that attracts the user. For this, create an intro that attracts the user. Keep in mind that you do not intentionally make the video too long, and keep in mind that your video is giving the user a good idea of what they are looking for. Note that you use simple words in the video. And if you are recording the video with your voice then try to display your full energy in the video. You can show something in the video that will catch the attention of the user. Always try to show them something new and tell them.

3. Create a playlist

If you create a playlist associated with a relevant topic, then if the user likes a video of your channel, he may also see the other video on your playlist. It also helps in increasing the ranking of the video. For example, let's say you are creating a tutorial related to something that you have done many parts of, then collect all parts of it and create a playlist, so users will like to see the playlist you have created again if they liked it. And the more time a user spends on your channel's video, the more your channel's watch time will increase.

4. Use video cards on the last screen

YouTube's last screen helps a lot in increasing the watch time of any YouTube channel. It's like a video hyperlink that you can show in the last. The last screen of YouTube Video is a frame that you can use as a call to action to show more videos to the user at the end of the video or to motivate the user to watch more videos. Here you can give a link to the next part of the video or create a poll to know the intentions of people. This also makes the video a little attractive and also helps in increasing the watch time.

5. Customize your video title

As you also know, YouTube is a search engine, so search engine optimization (SEO) is also necessary for your video. When selecting a video to show in the search result, YouTube's algorithm takes into account many elements. And for that, you need to do some optimization. This includes the title, description and tag of the video. The information related to it along with the video, which you have mentioned in the video, must also be mentioned in its title and description. Also, use the keyword in the title and description on which you want to rank the video. Also, if you have used some copyrighted items in the video, then give credit for it.

6. Optimize your channel

If any user comes to your YouTube channel and if he is looking for other videos on your channel, then he will visit your channel. In such a situation, keeping your channel optimized, i.e. your channel should have the right profile photo, banner, etc.

Along with this, it is also necessary to have social media links, websites, descriptions, etc. so that the user can easily know what kind of video you post on your channel.

Note that your profile photo should be 800 x 800 pixels. It should look good when viewed in a shorter format. Your cover image should be at least 2560 x 1440 pixels. Also, the description of your channel, which is displayed in the Information tab, should be 1000 characters. Make sure to use keywords in the description so that your channel is easily visible in the search result.

7. Make eye-catching thumbnail

The video thumbnail is the one that appears as an image with the video when the video is searched. A good and eye-catching Thumbnail will help increase the click-through rate of your videos which will also increase the ranking of your videos. And if the ranking increases, the watch time of your video will also increase. When uploading a video, an auto-generated thumbnail appears, instead creating a differently-designed thumbnail.

When designing Thumbnail, keep in mind that it contains the mentions of the things that you are going to tell in the video. Keep the background in bright colour. Also, put the watermark of your channel in the Video Thumbnail. Keep in mind that the things included in Thumbnails should be such that they can catch the user's attention.

Keep the following things in mind when making a thumbnail.

- Thumbnail's aspect ratio should be 16:9.
- Keep the resolution of the thumbnail 1280 × 720.
- Create a file that is less than 2MB in size.
- To Thumbnail. JPG, GIF, BMP or. Format as PNG.

Promote your videos on other social channels

If you have other social media followers, every time you upload a new video to YouTube, let it know to your followers. You can also embed your YouTube videos on your website into blog posts and pages. This will help more and more people to watch your videos and hopefully you get more and more watch time on your YouTube video.

If you don't already have social media followers, then start creating followers by creating an account on social media. By doing this, your YouTube channel will become popular in a very short time.

Upload videos regularly

Let's make a mistake for every new YouTuber. They will not upload regular videos on their channel. Many people, after uploading videos for some time, lose the desire to create and upload videos when views are not found. And, they get frustrated. But that's their biggest mistake. YouTube won't trust your channel until you do something good. YouTube takes time to trust your new channels and videos. So forget everything and just keep making good videos and upload videos 3 to 4 days a week on any given day. If the content and quality of your videos are good, people and YouTube will love your channel and video.

Just remember, if you're getting to see the video, don't be discouraged. Just keep making good videos and upload videos on a regular channel. The result will soon be in front of your eyes.

CHAPTER NINE

WHAT CAN GOOGLE ASSISTANT DO FOR YOU?

Today, those who have a mobile phone think of their mobile as their friend and they want to talk to him. And today mobile is the only thing that is the best means of inspiring people's minds. Nowadays, people prefer such mobiles in which Google Assistant can be used. That means they can talk to him. There are a lot of people who ask a variety of questions to Google Assistant, one of the same questions is what can you do?

In this chapter, I'm going to answer the "What can you do" question. However, when you use Google Assistant, you should know what Google Assistant can do? Because in answer to this question, the answer to your question is hidden. Many people search in Google by not asking the same question to Google Assistant. So you just read this chapter, after all the doubts related to your questions, what can you do will be cleared.

What can you do? (What Google Assistant can do?)

Google Assistant is a digital assistant that can understand your voice or answer the questions you ask. It can control your entire device by staying in your device. That is, when you say ok google what you can do, you will get the answer to this question immediately. Also you can ask any question or give it an order like play a song on YouTube, or tell a good joke. It's always ready at your service.

When you ask Google Assistant what you can do, they may not be able to give a full answer. That's why here we understand you in the language of Google Assistant what it can do.

1. I can control your device and your smart home appliances.
2. I can give details of online guidelines, weather, news, nearby restaurants, etc.
3. I can play the song.
4. I can tell you the information related to the calendar.
5. I can set up an appointment.
6. I can open the message and make a call.
7. I can open apps on your phone.
8. I can set up a timer and reminder for you.
9. I can read the notice for you.
10. I can book tickets or hotels online and tell you the flight timings.

Not only that, there are many more tasks that Google Assistant can do. If you are going to use it for the first time or you have not used it then you will find its features very attractive.

Ok Google, what can you do? What can Google Assistant do for you?

Google Assistant is able to understand your points and answer commands or questions. It is similar to Apple's Siri, Microsoft's Cortana and Amazon's Alexa. It answers all your questions in your own way.

If any smartphone already has a Google Assistant activated, then in front of that device you will speak Ok Google, then Google Assistant will immediately become active and listen to the words you say. Simply put, you can ask anything from Google Assistant by saying Ok Google. Like bring the phone closer to you and say "Ok Google what can you do". Your questions will be answered immediately thereafter.

Ok, apart from speaking Google, if you keep pressing the Home button on your smartphone for a little longer, you can still activate the Google Assistant. You can then ask questions by clicking on the Mic icon.

Can you call?

Many people also want to know if Google Assistant can make a call or not. The answer to this question is a bit complicated. Do you mean to say Google should call you? So it is not possible. But Google Assistant can definitely call someone from your device. For this, you can give him the voice command "Ok Google, call (Name)". After this you do nothing, according to what you say, the call will start connecting.

Can you love?

People also want to know from Google Assistant whether they can love it or not. People think that someone is talking to them, that is, a girl is talking to them. But it's your mistake, Google Assistant has been created because of this so that it can talk to you in your style. He's not someone who can love anyone. But she can definitely answer your questions in different ways so that you will also like to talk to her. But it is clear that you can't love Google Assistant.

Other questions related to what you can do

Can you sing a song?

Google Assistant can't sing itself, but it can definitely play any song on Google or YouTube for you.

Can you marry me?

Google Assistant is just a service that can talk to you, and understand what you say. He is not a person, nor is there any emotion in him. Google Assistant can't marry you.

What do you eat?

Google Assistant has been created by Google's engineers to talk to you and answer your questions. It just needs an internet connection and a little bit of electricity to run.

Where do you live?

When you ask Google Assistant where you live, you will get the answer that it lives on your device. There is no special place to stay, it is a service that is offered in every Android smartphone nowadays.

CHAPTER TEN

WHAT IS A BLOG?

Before we know the answers to these questions, let's talk about some interesting statistics related to it:

- By October 2011, Statista said about 173 million blogs had been created worldwide.
- Now according to an estimate, the number of blogs on the entire internet has exceeded 44 crores.
- More than 700 million posts are written on these blogs every month.
- Every month, more than 400 million people like you and I read these blogs, even if we are not aware of them.

What is a blog?

Blog means a type of website that people use as a digital diary and on it, they share their experience, their thoughts and information with people through text, images, videos, etc. The blog was initially called a weblog.

What is a blog post?

The content of the blog is called a blog post. And there can be a lot of blog posts in one blog. The blog post is shown in an order according to the date of updating, in which new posts are shown earlier and old posts are shown later.

The blog can also be kept private so that other people can't see it. But most of the blogs on the internet are public which anyone can read. A blog is run by one person or a team. Now they have stepped into the world of big corporate blogging and they share a lot of content on their blogs for this work they keep a whole team of many people.

Blog posts can be shared on social media such as Facebook, Twitter, WhatsApp, etc. Most blogs have a comment section at the bottom of every article (post) in which anyone can express their opinion about that content. Now blogging is seen as a business and people have started making careers in it.

History of Blogging

- **1994:** An American student named Justin Hall created the world's first blog links.net on which he used things related to his personal life as a diary.
- **1997:** The term "weblog" was first used by Jorn Barger, the editor of a blog called Robot Wisdom.
- **1998:** Bruce Abelson, a computer programmer and website developer, created an open diary. On which the user could write a diary on which the first comment system was also added with the privacy setting.
- **1999:** Peter Merholz shortened the word weblog to blog, and that's where the word blog began. This year, Pyra Labs created the first blog platform Blogger where people could write blogs without coding.

- **2003:** Google bought Blogger and Adsense. This year Matt Mullenweg launched WordPress.
- **2007:** Tumblr was launched which gave rise to the concept of micro-blogging. Now people could share not only text but also images, videos, GIFs, etc. Even people could publish posts via SMS and email. It was the world's fastest-growing social platform, which yahoo later bought in 2013 for $1.1 billion.
- **From 2007 to the present:** Now the scope of blogging has increased, it has increased, it has come out of a diary and almost every business is social media platforms like Facebook, Twitter, WhatsApp and Instagram, which can be connected to the blog and reach more and more people.

Why do people do blogging? What are the benefits of creating a blog?

There are many benefits to creating a blog and different people do blogging for their different benefits. Many people aim to earn money from it, so many people start a blog to help others.

The advantages of a blog are many and there can be many purposes behind creating people's blogs such as:

- to express your thoughts
- to share your information
- To create an online portfolio to get a new job
- To earn money online
- To earn a name
- To advance the business
- To master your field

- It makes you a better writer.
- To create a network
- to help others.
- to learn from others.

What do you call a blogger? How many types are there?

The creator and the one who writes on it is called a blogger. A blog can also be run by one or more people.

There are many types of bloggers which we have divided into mainly four parts:

1. Amateur Blogger:

People who share information related to their hobbies on their blogs are called amateur bloggers. They talk about the topic they are interested in. A good hobby blogger pays more attention to his content and its quality and not to money. The speciality of this type of blogging is that people stay connected to their blog for a long time and do not get frustrated even if they do not get money from the blog because they are writing on their favourite topic.

2. Part-time Blogger:

Job seekers, college or school-going students can also do blog writing in their free time. The advantage of this is that the time is utilised and some money is also received in return. However, in the beginning, it is not easy to earn money from a blog, it will take you a lot of time to do so. But if you need money immediately, then you can also earn money by writing articles for another blogger in your free time.

3. Full-time blogger:

Believe me, there are many people whose main source of income is the blog. Such people spend all their time blogging and are constantly creating quality content for their audience. The traffic on their site gradually increases and then they earn money through advertisements and different ways.

4. Professional Blogger:

They are also full-time bloggers but they work for a corporate or an institution and their main job is to promote the brand and bring in new customers or clients for the business. They mostly write information related to the company's product or service on their blog and try to reach as many people as possible.

What's the job of a blogger?

A blogger does not just have to write an article to run his blog successfully but also has to do a lot of other things like:

- Planning and setting goals for blogs
- Research for articles
- Edit the image if you need to select the right image for the blog post
- Designing your blog if needed
- Fix site speed and other problems

- Create fan pages on Facebook and other platforms for your blog
- Sharing blog posts on different social media platforms
- Optimize your top blog posts
- Replying to comments and deleting spam comments
- Reading other people's blogs and learning from there
- Guest posting means writing posts on others' blogs
- Establishing relationships with other bloggers and supporting each other
- Finding ways to monetize your blog in advertising, sponsorship and other ways
- Setting up a newsletter
- Analyzing traffic and other data
- Staying in touch with your audience
- Make plans to reach out to more and more people

Just as it takes a lot of work to advance a business, it takes a lot of effort to make a blog successful.

How many types of blogs are there? On which topic is the blog written?

There are millions of blogs in this world and there are many topics on which something is being written daily. But at the time of starting a blog, many people are worried about what kind of blog they should create and what kind of content to post on it.

First of all, we have to choose a topic which is also called niche and then information related to it is posted.

If we want, we can also write on more than one topic.

There are many types of blogs and depending on the topic, we can divide it into many parts such as:

- fashion
- Food
- Fitness
- new
- Lifestyle
- sport
- film
- Gaming
- Finance
- Politics
- business
- Personal
- Automobile
- domestic animal

If you are also thinking of creating a blog, then our advice would be to start writing on your favourite topic. You can write on more than one topic if you want.

Can you make money from a blog?

Yes! You can earn money by blogging and a lot of people are also earning. But just as it takes planning and hard work to earn money from a business, in the same way, it is also planned and constantly worked hard to earn a good income from a blog.

There are many ways to monetize a blog, some of which are the most commonly used are as follows:

- advertisement
- Affiliate Marketing
- Selling your goods or services
- from donation

- By propagating your own business

Apart from this, nowadays people are also earning online through CPA marketing, for this, the blogger has to register on the site of the CPA affiliate from where the advertisement received has to be put on his site and through this, money is received when the product is sold or if the lead is generated. One such site is Dr Cash which is a CPA network and affiliate marketing of products related to beauty and health (Nutra vertical).

To earn money by blogging, good traffic is required on the blog, for which a blogger has to work very hard. If you want traffic from Google, you should also be aware of SEO.

Who can do blogging?

Blogging doesn't require any special ability. This can be done by any class of people by taking time out such as:

- school student
- College Student
- Housewife (Housewife)
- person who does the job

Every person who has something to write about can do blogging. He just needs to have some information about the internet and blogging.

What do you need to create a blog?

Before you start, you have to decide on which topic you can create articles or content on. After this, you have to create a platform where you can post your article. For this, you will need two things:

- Domain Name
- Web Hosting

A domain name means a web address through which your blog can be viewed. You have to buy an address which is called a domain name. For this, you can take 99 rupees to 1500 rupees. There are many websites from which you can buy domains such as:

- GoDaddydy
- big rockck
- Namecheapip

After this, you will need web hosting, which will give you a space on the internet where you will be able to upload your content. For hosting, you have to pay some money monthly or annually depending on which hosting provider you use. You'll find a lot of hosting providers on the Internet such as:

- Bluehost
- HostGator
- Hostinger

If you do not want to spend money on hosting, then you can use Blogger.com which is a free blogging platform of Google. Although it has many limitations, it is useful for beginners.

We can call a blog a type of digital diary that exists as a website on the internet. On this, we can write down our thoughts or information on a topic and share it with people.

But a blog doesn't just mean sharing your thoughts, you can also make money from the blog and run it as a business. Nowadays, many people are blogging and taking advantage of it. You can also create a blog of your own if you want.

CHAPTER ELEVEN

HOW TO START A BLOGGING CAREER?

Many people like to write and complete their art of writing through a book or post. All writers are writers, but not all writers are bloggers. Now let's know how to earn money from blogging.

Here we are talking about bloggers when we write about a topic and explain all its information in our own way. After that, all the information on the subject is uploaded to the website as a post. All this work is called blogging. How to start a blogging career step by step in 2022 When we search for a topic on Google, Google provides us with all the information related to that topic. Where does all this information come from on Google? All this information is the same as what the blogger writes on the website through his post. Today we will learn how to create a blog for free and make money. If you also want to earn money from blogging, read this chapter.

How to start a blogging career?

Here we will tell you step by step how you can make a career in blogging. How to write a good blog and how to earn online income for yourself from here. All the information you are going to get ahead, if you stay with us, then let's start.

Let me tell you that blogging can be started in two ways, one in which you will not spend a single penny. That's where everyone starts blogging. It is absolutely free, Google has its own platform which name is Blogger.

The second medium is WordPress where you have to spend money to get the domain name and buy hosting to run the website.

Here we will explain to you both ways what are the advantages and disadvantages of blogging on Free Blogger. The second can run your website well by blogging on WordPress.

How to start blogging on Blogger?

First of all, you have to do logging on to the blogger from your mail ID, then go to the Google app and open the blogger, after the blogger is opened, you have to choose the name for the blog.

After selecting the name, the address for the blog, which is called domain, has to be selected, you have to choose the domain name related to whichever topic you want to create the blog on.

How to get a domain name on Blogger?

First of all, you have to go to the blogger from your mail ID to the blogger, you have to keep the name of your blog there. When selecting the name, keep in mind that select the name that is similar to the subject you want to work in or create a blog. Every blog has its own identity. And google search is also easy.

Let me tell you that the domain name here is available with blogspot.com which is absolutely free. For example, suppose you want to create a blog on cooking, then the name related to it can be such that Specialfood.blogspot.com it will be the URL of our blog. Through this, the visitor will reach our website.

Now you must have understood how the domain name is taken on blogger and what kind of it is.

Do you need a theme on Blogger?

It is very important to apply the theme, by applying the theme, our website gets a great look, which we can also customize according to our own so that our visitors stay on our website for a longer time.

For the theme, we do not have to spend anything separately on the blogger itself, we get a theme better than one. Let me tell you that the theme should be something that the visitor can easily understand and does not have any problem in opening the website.

Post on Blogger?

After putting the domain name and theme, now it is the turn to write a post related to whatever topic you have thought of creating your blog on. Each post should have at least 1500 words.

The post should be in such a way that contains all the information related to the topic. The visitor does not feel that the post is incomplete. That is to say, the visitor should get some value from the post.

Posts should not be copy-pasted from anywhere, whatever you write, write in your own way. To make the post look good, put the photo related to the post in it. Putting up posts with the photo makes the reader feel good, the person will not be bored and will stay for a long time.

Put an internal link in the post because when a person is reading the post, then he can go to the next post related to that post.

How to start blog writing?

In today's time, blogging has become very easy, earlier people used to consider blogging to be very difficult because earlier people used to do blogging in English, just as its trend in India increased, since the blog started becoming Hindi and Google also started supporting it. To create a blog in Hindi, you have to choose your language Hindi. Hindi can have the option of extension to typing to change the language of typing.

Website Pages:

At the top of the blog, there should be **contact us, about us, terms and conditions, privacy policy** and **disclaimer** pages. It's important to search on Google.

Contact us is so important that when someone is reading a post, he can contact us if he has to ask a question or if someone wants to do his work through our post.

You have to give information about and about yourself about the blog within us. All the information on which topic our post will be written has to be put inside it.

Terms and conditions, privacy policy and disclaimers can be made from the software.

How to Blogging on WordPress?

To blog on WordPress, it is necessary to take a custom domain, here the domain with Blogspot does not work. Custom domains such as .com .in .org domains are used.

The domain name is provided to us by the hosting company for which we have to pay the charges annually. If we take premium hosting then the first year it gets free.

What is Web Hosting?

People who do blogging prefer to work with web hosting. Web hosting hosts our website. The speed of the blog is good, and the safety of the blog is also there. It also offers the facility of backup for the website. Jog people come to your site, if the website opens late, then close it and go to another website, then the ranking of your blog decreases. That's why it's important to take web hosting. For web hosting, we have to drink a few amounts of money annually.

How to install WordPress?

Now after taking domain and hosting, WordPress has to be installed, to install WordPress, you will find the WordPress installer in the dashboard of the hosting itself, with the help of which it becomes very easy to install. For WordPress, we don't have to pay any separate charges.

Plugin feature in WordPress

WordPress also gives us the feature of plugins that make it easier to create a website and write posts using it. This feature is not in Blogspot.

Here the plugin gets two types of plugins, one is the free one, the other for which we have to pay the charges.

We've mentioned about pages, themes and posts above.

Post to bring in the ranking by doing SEO

After writing the post, he has to do SEO (Search Engine Optimization) to lane in the true engine. That is to say, the post has to be written well so that the post can come easily in Google search. Use the right words, and make the senses correctly. Enter the keyword correctly so that Google can easily search for your post.

After completing all these tasks, you can apply for Google Adsense. There are some rules of Google Adsense, and on fulfilling them, you get the approval of AdSense, after which you can earn the earnings of your website.

So now he knows. Blogging full information 2022 on how to start your career with blogging. What things do we have to take care of for blogging? All the information has been shared one by one above. I hope you understand the information.

CHAPTER TWELVE

WHAT IS A DOMAIN NAME?

Whenever you searched for a website, you must have encountered a domain name. It must have come to your mind what is the relationship between a website and a domain name. So let me tell you that with the help of a domain name, we can search the website on the internet. We can say that this is a friendly naming system by which we can provide the address of a web page and web server.

I know that you will also have some information about what the domain is, so I thought why not give you all the information about the domain name in today's time so that there is no more confusion among you people?

What is a domain?

A domain name or DNS (Domain Naming System) is a naming that allows us to identify a website on the Internet. Talking about any website, all backgrounds are connected to some IP address. The IP address (Internet Protocol Address) is a numerical address that tells the browser where the website is located on the Internet.

In simple language, we humans remember easy things, in the same way, all websites also have a name, so now you can think that a domain name is the easier name that we can remember that any IP address. This is a human-readable version of the IP address.

With the help of domain names, we can find one or more IP addresses. The domain name google.com example refers to hundreds of IPs. Domain names are also used in URLs to visualize a particular webpage.

How the domain name works

I want to tell you that all websites are hosted or stored on one server. And the domain name is pointed to the IP of that server.

Whenever you add a website's name to your URL bar, it points to your server's IP with the help of your domain name so that you can see your searched website in your browser. That's how you see the website.

Type of Domain:

Domain names are very similar, but today I will tell you about all the types of very important people. So that whenever you choose a domain name, it is very easy for you to choose it.

1. TLD – Top Level Domains

Top Level Domains (TLDs) are also known as Internet Domain Extensions. This is the last part where the domain name ends. Part of the latter part of the dot. It was first developed. With the help of this domain, you can easily rank your website. It's very SEO friendly. And the Google search engine also gives it more importance.

Example of TLD Extension that anyone can buy

- .com (commercial)
- .org (organization)
- .net (network)
- gov (government)
- .edu (education)
- .name (name)
- .biz (business)
- .info (information)

e.g. Google.com, Facebook.com etc.

2. CcTLD – Country Code Top Level Domains

This type of domain is commonly used by keeping a particular country in mind. It is named based on a country's two-letter ISO code. For example, there are some important domain extensions.

- .us: United States
- .in: India
- .ch: Switzerland
- .cn: China
- .ru: Russia
- .br: Brazil

What is a subdomain name?

You may have known what the domain is, but the subdomain is a part of your main domain name. The subdomain is not purchased. If you have purchased any top-level domain name, you can divide it into subdomain names. It's free, you don't have to pay any charge for it.

Note: Mainly all American servers use three-letter top-level domains (e.g. ".com", ".edu"). But other countries use only two letters or combinations of two letters other than America. (e.g ".au", ".ca", ".co.jp").

The domain name and URL are not the same

If you talk technically, the domain name is a small part of the larger internet address called the "URL". In the URL, we can find out many things compared to domain names such as specific page address, folder name, machine name, and protocol language.

For example, the URL (Uniform Resource Locator pages) has been boldened to their domain name:

- https://**xyz.in**/what-is-domain-name/
- http://www.**abcdefg.com**/2022/07/20/books/digital-media.html

Top Domain Name Provider List

If you want to create a website for yourself or your business, then you can also buy a domain name yourself, but for that, you have to register an account in the domain from a good domain name service provider and buy a new and unique domain name. Below I have given a list of some of the top domain providers for your convenience. You can choose any of these.

- Bigrock
- GoDaddy
- Namecheap
- 1and1
- ZNetLive
- EWeb Guru

• IPage

Note: ICANN (The Internet Corporation for Assigned Names and Numbers) is an organization that authorizes these domain providers to sell domain names.

How to create a domain name

- Always choose a short domain name that is easy to remember.
- Have a domain name that is easy to remember, type, and speak.
- Do not have a domain name similar to any other and be unique so that you can easily brand.
- Do not keep special characters such as hyphens and numbers in this name as possible.
- Always try to take top-level domains that everyone in the whole world recognizes.
- Your domain name should be related to or similar to your business or business profile, which will make it easier for you to create a brand.
- In Aqir, I want to tell you that the domain name should always be a short and easily remembered address. The technical address of the server is IP (Internet Protocol Address).

CHAPTER THIRTEEN

What is Web Hosting?

Any website needs web hosting to show it on the internet. If you are going to build a website or you have to know how to make a website then you should also have information about web hosting.

Today we will learn in this article what is web hosting. how many types are these? how does it work? What are its features? What's the difference between hosting and domain? beginning

What is Web Hosting?

When you create a website or blog, all its contents such as images, videos, pages, etc. have to be stored on the server so that other people can access it through the internet. Web hosting is a type of service that allows us to upload our website to the Internet. For website hosting, we need a powerful server that should always be connected to the Internet so that our website is available to users 24 hours a day without any problems. Since we cannot maintain this type of server ourselves because its maintenance cost is very high, we resort to web hosting companies for website hosting. Web hosting companies have powerful servers, technology, and technical staff. We buy a hosting service from them according to the monthly or annual package and we find space in their servers where we can easily host our website.

How many types of web hosting are there?

There are also many types of web hosting, when we create a website, we buy hosting according to our needs. There are mainly 4 types:

- Shared
- Dedicated
- VPS
- Cloud

Now let's understand these in a little detail:

Shared Hosting:

As the name suggests, in this type of hosting, many websites are using the same server. Since, you are using multiple websites together with the space, RAM, and CPU of the same server, it will be much cheaper for you than another hosting. Just like if you use your car to go somewhere, you will have to spend more money, but if you travel by bus, you will be saved a lot of money. If the crowd on the bus becomes more during the journey, then you may have problems, in the same way, there may be some problems sometimes in shared hosting.

For example, if the traffic on your website comes too much, then the speed of the website will be reduced and your visitors may start seeing some technical errors.

Shared hosting is best for:

If your business is small or you are just starting then this type of hosting is much better for you. If you are creating a blog then you should start with shared hosting. It is very easy to host a website in shared hosting. You can easily install many tools and plugins.

Dedicated Hosting:

You have the right to the entire server. It has many advantages, but it is very expensive compared to another hosting. Since only your website is being hosted on the entire server, it is completely under your control. You can make changes to its operating system and other settings.

One of the advantages of dedicated hosting is that you can avoid the damage caused by more traffic. This increases the speed and performance of your website.

Dedicated hosting is best for:

Websites that have a lot of traffic should take dedicated hosting. If you have an eCommerce website whose size is very large, then it will be a very good hosting for you.

VPS (Virtual Private Server) Hosting:

We can understand VPS hosting as a mix of both shared and dedicated hosting. In this model, you have a dedicated server but this server is a virtual server and not a physical server, let's understand in a little detail:

Here a server is divided into several different virtual servers. A virtual server is given for a website and only he has the right to that part.

Here, a website gets more space, computing power and bandwidth than shared hosting, so in VPS hosting, the page load time becomes faster than the shared hosting.

It is not better than dedicated hosting, but it is better than shared hosting. If you think that there is going to be a lot of traffic on your site, then you should know that it also has some limitations in VPS hosting.

Who uses VPS hosting?

Small websites that get a small amount of traffic can also take advantage of VPS hosting. If you feel that the loading speed of your site is decreasing, you'd be better off choosing VPS hosting than shared hosting.

Cloud Hosting:

The problem with dedicated servers and VPS is that you have few resources, there is a limit on storage and capacity. Although most websites do not reach this limitation, sometimes some of the contents of the website can be viral and this suddenly leads to increased traffic which is difficult to handle. The solution to these problems can be found in cloud hosting. Here, there is no one server, but many servers together host your website.

In the last few years, cloud hosting has become very popular and its trend is increasing. The high volume of traffic on your site on cloud hosting does not affect its loading speed. However, you cannot control the entire server in it like dedicated hosting, i.e. you cannot change any server settings or install any special software. But if you have a simple website and you don't need more technical options, cloud hosting can be a good option for you.

Who uses cloud hosting?

Cloud hosting is a very flexible hosting solution. You can increase disk space and memory according to your need. It is perfect for organizations, apart from this, it is also very useful for subsite owners who are troubled due to traffic spikes from time to time.

How does web hosting work?

There are many companies for web hosting that allow website owners to host websites on their servers and in return take some money from you every month.

After uploading all the HTML pages, images, videos, etc. of the website to the server, anyone can view it through the internet anytime through the web address (domain name).

Whenever an internet user comes to your website by entering a web address in his web browser, his computer will be connected to the server where you have hosted the website. Now the server will display those HTML pages and contents on the visitor's browser.

What's the difference between web hosting and domain?

Domain names and web hosting are two different things. But many companies sell domains and hosting. For example – GoDaddy is the world's largest domain registrar, but it also offers the facility of hosting in addition to the domain.

New people are often confused between web hosting and domains.

If we put it in simple words:

"**A domain name is like your home address; while web hosting is like rooms of your home where you keep your belongings.**"

Here the address is the domain name which is the address of your website and for storage, computer hard disk, memory, etc. are used which recalled web hosting.

What are the features of hosting?

While buying hosting, you must keep in mind some of the basic features given below, these can also vary according to the hosting type, hosting company and plan.

- **Bandwidth:** Bandwidth refers to the amount of data that is being transferred between your website and visitors at a certain time. With more bandwidth, more and more people can access your website at the same time without any interruption, while low bandwidth can reduce the speed of your website.
- **Uptime:** This is one of the most important features of a reliable web hosting provider. Many companies offeguaranteeded uptime which means that your website will be available to their visitors for at least 99.per cent of the time.
- **Storage:** In every hosting account you should have enough disk space to store your web page, graphics, other media files, etc. You should choose the best hosting plan for yourself keeping in mind your needs.
- **Email:** You can take the facility of web hosting as well as email hosting in which you can create a custom email

address for yourself or your organization. In email hosting, you also have many other features from receiving demand ails, using emails, such as virus & spam filters, address calendarslander, etc.

- **Backups:** Sometimes some files are deleted from your computer and your data is lost. Keep in mind that the server is also a type of computer, there is a risk of data loss, so keep weathering whether your hosting providers are giving you the facility of backup or not.
- **Customer Support:** It's also very important, you should know whether your hosting provider is available for your technical assistance or not, can you call them? What time are they available? Can you tell them your problem by sending them an email? What is their response time? What is the feature of live chat? Do they have forums, tutorial articles, etc.? With these features, you can easily solve any problems related to upcoming hosting in the future.

CHAPTER FOURTEEN

BLOGGER VS WORDPRESS – WHICH ONE TO CHOOSE?

So all our new blogger brothers always have a problem, I also had the same problem that after all, it would be right to choose which platform is Blogger or WordPress, so in today's post, I will tell you Blogger vs. WordPress. They have platforms such as WIX, Tumblr, etc. for blogging and also from Bohot. But the two main platforms on which a professional website can be created are Blogger and WordPress. So these two platforms are the most commonly used. Both platforms have different features and disadvantages too. But in one more thing, it is clear that it also depends on which platform is right.

So in this chapter, I will give you the full details of both the platforms, what are advantages or what disadvantages, we will talk about all the things, then by the end, we will read the whole article.

What is Blogger?

So friends, as I told you earlier, Blogger.com blogging is a great platform for blogging, here you can start your own blog. And the best thing about this platform is that it is a product of Google, so you will not have any kind of problem.nIn this platform, you get everything on the dashboard, such as a theme editor or all the other important things. The good thing is that if you have the knowledge of HTML (Hyper Text Markup Language) even a little bit, then you can easily customize it. And the biggest point due to which this platform is used the most is that it's a free service where you can start the website for absolutely free.

You will also find the domain here for free, but it will also have blogspot.com. Let's say you selected multigyan, then the domain you will get for free will be multigyan.blogspot.com

And it is not that the hosted site does not rank on the blogger, you can see if you can do the research yourself. You can also put your own custom domain on blogger. So if you want to create a website from blogger, then it will cost you only to take the domain. But if you don't want to do that too, then you get the domain for free.

Blogger Pros:

- If you use blogger, then you do not need to take hosting, you can live your website on the internet without hosting.

- You can take as many domains as you want for free. And it is also not that they do not rank the domain, blogger's domain also comes in the top-level domain.
- For Blogger, you will get online themes for free, through which you can easily create a professional blog or website.
- The hosted site on Blogger is never down no matter how much traffic it takes.
- Here you do not need to take an SSL certificate, you get the option to enable it for free in Blogger's dashboard.

Blogger Cons:

- If you create a website on Blogger, then you must have knowledge of HTML because it is based on the whole HTML.
- Now because Blogger is based on HTML, you do not get the option to install any kind of plugin here, you have to implement anything by coding.
- In Blogger, you can't change your site the whole way. Like the URL etc., you don't get the options of everything in it anywhere.
- On Blogger, you don't get to see customer support as good as you get on WordPress.
- A professional website cannot be created on Blogger compared to WordPress. Because bloggers don't have plugins installed or premium themes.

What is WordPress?

So let's talk about what is WordPress? WordPress is a great and most usable blogging platform where you can create your own professional website or blog. If you see, there are more advantages to WordPress than Blogger because you can design a blog, and change or create things as you wish here.

Whether you have HTML knowledge or not, you can do customization directly. And because you get the option to install plugins, then you can add things that will make your website great. And so because you can install many plugins, then if you install SEO plugins on your website, then you can think that you will get more help in SEO.

Now because WordPress gives you so much saree best facility, then you will have to pay something. You don't have to buy WordPress, but you have to purchase hosting. And you have to take the domain. Online you will find many saree hosting companies which provide you with hosting at cheap cost and also give the best services. So you can install WordPress from there using those hosting. Before that, you have to purchase the domain and connect it to the hosting.

WordPress Pros:

- In WordPress, you can install plugins. With the help of this, you can add different kinds of things to your blog or website and this will also benefit you in SEO.
- If you use WordPress, even if you do not have the knowledge of HTML, you can do full customization without worrying about it.
- It's easy to do the menu or other customization in WordPress.

- If you have any kind of trouble or problem in your WordPress panel, then you can talk about their customer support or your hosting provider's customer support.
- WordPress's site ranks quickly rather than a blogger's site. Now it is not that the hosted site on Blogger does not rank at all, but there is a little difference.

WordPress Cons:

The biggest con is that you can't use WordPress for free. You have to purchase both hosting and domain only then you will be able to use it.

In WordPress, you get storage according to hosting, which means that you can store as much data as you have been given in your hosting plan. But bloggers don't have that you can store as much data as you want. But if you buy a good hosting plan, then you get the option of unlimited storage in it.

Blogger V/S WordPress:

So friends, as you read about both Blogger and WordPress and also seen some of their Pros and Cons, then you will understand a little bit about which is a much better platform. WordPress without a doubt. But before that, we have to compare both the platforms in a little more detail. So let's now point to point out all the things about Blogger vs. WordPress.

Installation

Talking about installation, Blogger is the winner. Because in WordPress, first you have to purchase hosting, then install WordPress and setup, then a little things become more, but not at all difficult. There is nothing like this in Blogger, just you have to create an account and start writing articles by uploading the theme. So blogger is better in terms of installation.

Cost

In terms of cost, blogger vs. WordPress is the winner here. Because as I told you earlier that you have to purchase a separate hosting for WordPress, then you can use WordPress and you have to take the domain, then in the case of WordPress, the cost is a little more. Blogger doesn't have to do that just you have to connect the domain, and you don't have to buy some hosting.

Control

Blogger is also great in terms of control here. Because you don't get many things on Cookie Blogger and because you don't need to connect to cookie hosting, then you don't need to manage that too. But that's not the case in WordPress at all. You also have to maintain the hosting with WordPress, but once you have learned, then there is no more difficult task.

Features

Features are the most important points and the winner of this point is WordPress without any doubt. Because in WordPress you get the most features so that you can push your blog or website or say and make it better. Such as the feature of plugins etc. Blogger doesn't have that you don't get many features. Simply get a layout, you have to work on it. Coding is the only way to change or implement.

Security

In terms of security also, you will get the best WordPress and WordPress is the winner because in WordPress you can use many types of plugins, then you can install plugins for some security on it and use them easily. Blogger does not install any kind of plugins, so you do not get to see any kind of security in it.

Storage

In the case of storage, blogger can be the winner here, it is not even meant to say that there is no doubt that you get unlimited storage in Blogger, but you can also get unlimited storage in WordPress. If you buy a good plan hosting. In some plans, there is no unlimited hosting and in some, then you can take any plan according to your need.

Support

In the case of support here, we can say that WordPress is great because you get contact support from WordPress and from there you get a reply quickly. And you can also talk to your hosting provider if you have any problems. But the contact support you get in Blogger, you do not get a reply so quickly, but it is also not that you will not be helped on it.

Backup

In WordPress, you get the option of automatic backup. It either comes with your hosting plan or you can also do it with the help of the plugin Wagah. WordPress is the best in terms of backup. But if you talk about Blogger, then here you have to take a backup manually. But his method is also not very difficult, you can easily get backup in blogger.

SEO

Seo i.e. search engine optimization there is no doubt that WordPress is better. And this is the most important point for the blogger. Due to plugins, SEO's work becomes easy in WordPress, which increases the chances of ranking. But due to the absence of the option of plugins in blogger, blogger is left behind, but again I will say that it is not even this, the blogger's site does not rank. You just have to take care of everything.

CHAPTER FIFTEEN

WHAT IS SEO?

What is SEO and why is it important for a blog? The simple answer is that SEO is the life of blogging. Because no matter how good an article you want, if your article is not ranked properly, then the chances of traffic coming in it are negligible. In such a situation, all the hard work of the writers goes into the water.

In today's digital age, if you have to come in front of people, then online is the only way where you can be present in front of millions of people at the same time. Here, you can present yourself through videos or you can reach out to people through your written content. But to do this, you have to come to the first pages of search engines because these are the pages that visitors like and trust more.

But getting here is not that easy because for this you have to SEO your articles properly. This means that they have to be optimized in the right way so that they can be ranked in the search engine. And its process is called SEO. In today's article, we will get information about what is SEO and how to do it.

What is SEO?

SEO or search engine optimization is a technique by which we bring our posts or pages to the top, or rank on, any search engine. We all know what a search engine is. When it comes to search engines, let me tell you for your information, Google is the most popular search engine in the whole world, in addition to this, there are other search engines like Bing and Yahoo. With the help of SEO, we can put our blog in the No.1 position on all search engines.

For example, suppose we go to Google and type any keyword and search, then all the content related to that keyword, shows you Google. All of the content that we see comes from different blogs.

The result that we see at the top is at the No.1 rank in Google, only then it has retained its place at the top. On No.1, it means that SEO has been used in that blog in a very good way so that it has more visitors and that is why that blog has become popular. SEO helps us to rank no.1 on Google. This is a technique that increases the number of visitors to your website by placing it at the top of the search engine's search result.

If your website is at the top of the search result, then internet users will first visit your site, which increases the chances of more and more traffic to your site and your income also starts to be good. It is very important to use SEO to increase the organic traffic on your website.

What is the full form of SEO?

The full form of SEO is "**Search Engine Optimization**".

Why is SEO important for blogs?

You know what SEO is, now let's know why it is important for a blog. We use SEO to make our website accessible to people. Let's say I created a website, it also published good high-quality content, but if I don't use SEO, then my website will not be able to reach people and there will be no benefit to my website. If we do not use SEO, then whenever a user searches for a keyword, even if there is any content related to that keyword on your website, the user will not be able to access your website.

This is because the search engine will not be able to find your site nor will it be able to store the content of your website on its database. This will make it very difficult to have traffic to your website. Therefore, it is very important to do SEO correctly on your site. SEO is not so difficult to understand if you learn it, then you can make your blog much better and increase its value in the search engine.

After learning SEO, when you use it for your blog, you will not see its result immediately, so you have to be patient and do your work. Because the fruit of patience is sweet and you will see the colour of your hard work. As I have already said, how it becomes necessary to do SEO for ranking and traffic.

Why is SEO (Search Engine Optimization) so important?

Let's know more about the importance of search engine optimization:

- Most users use search engines on the Internet to answer their questions. In such a situation, they pay more attention to the top results shown by the search engine. So if you also want to come in front of people then you also have to take the help of SEO to rank the blog. That is, you have to come to the first page of the Google search result.

- SEO is not only for search engines, but having good SEO practices helps in increasing user experience and also increases the usability of your website.
- Users mostly trust the top results and this increases the trust of that website. Therefore, it is very important to know in the context of SEO, as well as to keep yourself updated.
- SEO is also very important for the social promotion of your website or blog. Because people who see your site in a search engine like Google, mostly share it on social media such as Facebook, Twitter, and Pinterest.
- SEO plays an important role in increasing the traffic of any site.
- SEO helps you to stay ahead in any competition. For example, if two websites are selling the same things, then the website that is SEO optimized attracts more customers and their sales also increase, while others are not able to do the same.

Types of SEO

There are two types of SEO, one is Onpage SEO and the other is Offpage SEO. The work of these two is completely different, let's know about them too.

- On-Page SEO
- Off-Page SEO

- Local SEO

What is on-page SEO?

On-page SEO works in your blog. This means designing your website properly that is SEO friendly. Follow the rules of SEO and use the template on your website. Writing good content and using good keywords in them that are most searched for in search engines. Using keywords in the right place on the page such as title, and meta description, and using keywords in the content makes it easier for Google to know who your content is written on top and helps to quickly rank your website on the Google page, which increases the traffic of your blog.

How to do on-page SEO?

Here we will learn about some techniques with the help of which we will be able to do our blog or website on-page SEO in a good way.

1. Website Speed

Website speed is a very important link from the point of view of SEO. A survey has found that any visitor stays on a blog or website for more than 5 to 6 seconds. If it does not open within this time, then he leaves it and migrates to another. And this thing also applies to Google because if your blog does not open quickly, then a negative signal reaches Google that this blog is not that good or it is not very fast. So keep your site speed as good as possible.

Here are some important tips that you can do to speed up your blog or website:

- Use simple and attractive themes
- Don't use too many plugins.
- Keep the size of the image to a minimum.
- Use the W3 Total Cache and WP Super Cache plugins

2. Navigation of the website

It should be easy to go around in your blog or website so that no visitor and Google have any problem moving from one page to another. The more comfortable the navigation of the website, the easier any search engine will be to navigate the site.

3. Title Tag

Make the title tag on your website very good so that if any visitor reads it, then click it on your title as soon as possible, it will also increase your CTR. How to create a good title tag: Do not use more than 65 words in your title because Google does not show the title tag in Google searches after 65 words.

4. URL of the post

Always keep the URL of your post as simple and short as you can.

5. Internal Link

This is a great way to rank your post. This allows you to interlink your related pages with each other. This allows all your interlinked pages to be easily ranked.

6. Alt Tag

Use images in your website's posts. Because you can get a lot of traffic from the images, so do not forget to put an ALT TAG in the image while using it.

7. Content, Heading and Keywords

As we all know about content, this is a very important link. Because content is also called king and the better your content, the better the valuation of the site. So write content for at least 800 words. This allows you to give complete information and it is also good for SEO. Never steal or copy content from anyone else.

Heading: You should take special care of the headings of your article as it has a lot of impact on SEO. The title of the article is H1 and you can nominate the subheadings after it with H2, H3, etc. With this, you must use the focus keyword.

Keyword: Use the LSI keyword when you type the article. This allows you to easily link people's searches. With this, bolden the important keywords so that Google and visitors know that these are important keywords and their attention will be attracted to them.

What is off-page SEO?

Off-page SEO is all about the blog. In off-page SEO, we have to promote our blog, like going to many popular blogs and commenting on their article and submitting a link to our website, we call it a backlink. Backlink benefits the website a lot. Create an attractive page of your website on social networking sites such as Facebook, Twitter, and Quora and increase your followers, this gives you the chance of increasing more visitors to your website. Submit a guest post to their blog that is very popular in the big blogs, so that the visitors to their blog will get to know you and traffic will start coming to your website.

How to do off-page SEO?

Here I will tell you about some off-page SEO techniques which will prove to be very useful for you in the long run.

- **Search Engine Submission:** Your website should be submitted to all search engines in the right way.
- **Bookmarking:** The pages and posts of your blog or website should be submitted to the bookmarking website.
- **Directory Submission:** Submit your blog or website to a directory with a popular high PR.
- **Social Media:** Create a page of your blog or website and profile on social media and link your website like Facebook, Twitter, LinkedIn
- **Classified Submission:** You should go to the Free Classified Website and advertise your website for free.
- **Q&A site:** You can go to the question and answer website and ask any question and link to your site.
- **Blog Commenting:** You can go to the related blog from your blog and comment on their posts and link your website (the link should be put up where the website is written)

- **Pin:** You can post the image of your website on Pinterest it is a very good way to increase traffic.
- **Guest Post:** You can go to the related blog from your website and do a guest post, it is the best place from where you can get a do-follow link and that too in the right way.

What is Local SEO?

Do people often ask what is local SEO? I believe the answer lies in the same question. If you merge local SEO, then these two words are a combination of local + SEO. That is, SEO done with a local audience in mind is called local SEO. It is a technique in which your website or blog is optimized especially so that it ranks better on the search engine for a local audience.

By the way, with the help of a website, you can target the whole internet, at the same time, if you have to target only one particular locality, then you have to use local SEO for this. In this, you have to optimize the name of your city, while its address details will also have to be optimized together. At the same time, to put it in a nutshell, then you have to optimize your site in such a way that people can get to know you not only online but also offline.

Example of Local SEO

- If you have a local business, such as a shop, where people come to visit you often, then if you optimize your website, there is something that can make it easier for people to reach you in real life.

- If here you target only one of your local areas and SEO optimized your site accordingly. This type of SEO is then called "local SEO".

Information about SEO terms

If you have a blog or a website, then you will know a lot about basic SEO, and how it works. But I know there are a lot of you who don't even know anything about basic SEO terms. So I thought why not give you some very important basic SEO terms so that you can also know about it?

Backlink

Also called its link or simply link, it is a hyperlink in another website that points to your website. Backlinks are very important from the point of view of SEO because they directly influence the search rankings of any webpage.

PageRank

PageRank is an algorithm that Google uses to predict which relative important pages are located on the web.

Anchor text

The anchor of any backlink is the type of text that is clickable. If your keyword is messed up in your anchor text, then it will also help you a lot from the SEO point of view.

Title Tag

Title Tag is primarily the title of any web page and this is a very important factor for Google's search algorithm.

Meta Tags

As soon as the title tag is used by the meta tag, search engines know what is in the content on the pages.

Search Algorithm

With the help of Google's search algorithm, we can find out which web pages are relevant throughout the Internet. About 200 algorithms work in Google's search algorithm.

SEP

Its full form is the **Search Engine Results Page**. It shows only those pages that are relevant to Google search engines.

Keyword Density

This keyword density shows how many times any keyword has been used in the article. Keyword density is very important from the point of view of SEO.

Keyword Stuffing

For example, I have already said that keyword density is very important from the point of view of SEO, but if a keyword is used more than necessary, it is called keyword stuffing. These are called negative SEO because it has a bad effect on your blog.

Robots.txt

It's not much but a file that's kept in the root of the domain. Using this, search boats are informed about the structure of the website.

What are organic and inorganic results?

There are two types of listings on the SERP (Search Engine Result Page) – Organic and Inorganic.

In this, for inorganic listing, we have to pay money to Google. That is, they are paid and have to pay money for it.

At the same time, an organic listing is completely free, i.e. without paying money, we can also come to the top page of Google, but for this, you have to do SEO first.

Is it easy to teach or do SEO?

There is no simple answer to that. Because one can never fully master SEO, it is because of the ever-changing changes in it. In such a situation, if you are serious about blogging, then you must keep the information about the SEO tutorial. By doing so, they are going to be of great use to you later. Seo does not have any rules, but they are based on some Google algorithms and it is constantly changing. One thing to keep in mind is that if someone tells you that he is a big SEO expert, then never believe him because to date no one has been able to be a master in SEO.

This is the only thing that is the case and it changes over time and according to the need. But still, there are some fundamentals of the Google SEO guide that are always the same. Therefore, bloggers must always keep themselves updated with the new SEO technology.

With this, you will know about the trends going on in the market, so that you can also make necessary changes in your articles, which will help you to rank later.

CHAPTER SIXTEEN

WHAT IS A URL ?

A URL is an acronym whose full form is "**Uniform Resource Locator**". You can think of it as a reference (or an address) that represents a unique resource on the Internet.

If you're new to the Internet, you'll find this word URL very confusing. You've probably heard about it here and there many times, but you won't know much about it. Then in today's article, you will get to know the full information about it.

What is the URL?

A URL is a formatted text string that is used to search for a network resource in a web browser, email clients, or any other software. Network resources can be any files such as web pages, text documents, graphics, or programs.

Since the resources are represented by the URL and the URL vertical, all of them are handled by the web server. In such a situation, it depends on the owner of that web server how to handle these resources and the URL associated with them.

How many parts of the URL are there?

There are three parts to any URL.

1. Protocol Designation
2. Host Name or Address
3. File or Resource Location

Special characters are used to distinguish all these substrings. The format of which is something like this.

protocol :// host / location

URL Protocol Substrings:

This type of protocol defines a network protocol so that a network resource can be easily accessed. These strings are often short names followed by three special characters ":":" This is a typical name conversion that denotes the protocol definition.

Typical protocols that are used are HTTP (http://), FTP (ftp://), etc.

URL Host Substrings:

With the help of the host substring, a destination computer or network device can be identified. Hosts come from standard Internet databases such as DNS and which we also know as IP addresses. The hostname of many websites does not just represent a single computer but it represents a group of web servers.

URL Location Substrings:

Location substring refers to the path of a particular network that is in that host. Resources reside primarily in a host directory or folder.

History of THE URL

Tim Berners-Lee was the first to bring this technology to the world about uniform resource locators. For the first time, he brought this idea to everyone's front that provides a unique locational address to all the web pages. So that they can be easily searched online. After creating HTML, a lot of pages were created on the World Wide Web using the standard language and hyperlinks with it. After that, the two of them were joined together. So that the internet became even bigger day by day.

How does the URL work?

The URL has been designed in such a way that it is easier for people to remember it. But the computer needs information to identify the right website so that it can easily find the right website. Our browser uses a webpage's IP to obscure it. IP is also known as internet protocol. These are a series of IP numbers which looks like 69.172.244.11

• *What is Web Hosting?*

Just imagine if we had to remember all the websites with their IP addresses, how difficult it would be for us to do this work. And the internet's desires are probably not as much as they are in this world today. Let me tell you that not all websites have static URLs. Some times change over time so it is a very difficult task to reach them. That's why we use URLs that are always the same and are also very easy to remember. When we type the URL of a website, the browser is also called DNS, also known as a domain name server, and with the help of this, it converts that URL to its corresponding IP. And with the help of which the browser reaches that website.

Types of URLs

By the way, there are many types of URLs and many different terms are used for them. I've mentioned some types here.

1. **Messy:** These are the types of URLs that contain a lot of numbers and letters that give an organization sense. For example, 'http://www.example.com/woeiruwoei909305820580'. From the common tor, these URLs are generated by computers that create thousands of web pages for a similar domain name.

2. **Dynamic:** These URLs also originated from the same place where the Messy URLs came from. These URLs are the result of a database query that provides content output in the result of any query. They also look similar to messy URLs that show characters like? &,%,+,=,$. They are mainly used on the website used by the consumer such as any shopping, or travelling websites in which the users change their queries frequently so that the answers are also changed.

3. **Static:** These are the exact opposite of any dynamic URL, this URL is completely hard-wired with the webpage's HTML coding. These URLs never change, no matter what the user is requesting.

4. **Obfuscated:** This is a very dangerous URL that is used in phishing scams. As its name suggests, they are hidden. Which is cleverly used so that it looks completely original. So when a user clicks it, he redirects them to the malicious

website.

Why characters are not used in URLs?

We all know that space is not used in URLs. But we should also know that according to RFC 1738, only alphanumeric characters and other characters such as !,$,-,_,*,',() are used in the string of the URL. And if any other characters are used, it has to be encoded.

Absolute versus Relative URLs

Absolute URLs are called those in which all the mentioned substrings are used. But in some cases only a few or one location element is used, such URLs are called relative URLs. Relative URLs are used in web servers and web pages as shortcuts to reduce the length of URL strings.

For example, the link to the same website is written in the format of relative URL and absolute URL.

Relative URL

<a href="/2016/September/word-of-the-day-04.htm">

Equivalent Absolute URL

<a href="http://thebestsiteever.com/2016/September/word-of-the-day-04.htm">

The best thing that happens is that with the help of the web server, all the missing protocols and host information are automatically filled. But keep in mind that relative URLs can only be used in places where host and protocol information can be established in advance.

What is URL Shortening?

If we talk about a modern website, then we will know that these are very long strings. And how difficult it is to share the strings of such a long URL. Many companies have created many such online translators with the help of which an absolute URL can be made very small and can be used wherever you want. There are some popular URL shorteners such as t.co for Twitter and lnkd.in (for LinkedIn). Along with this, there are many URL shortening services such as bit.ly and goo. gl with the help of which people around the world are shorting their URLs for free. Along with this, many URL shortening services and click statistics are also being offered. And some even check the malicious URL in the suspicious Internet domain and inform the user.

What are Secure URLs?

Secure URLs are websites that start with HTTPS://, the URL of such a website is called a secure URL. This means that even if you enter your personal information on such a website, it is encrypted before it is transmitted and it is not so easy to read it in favour of any hacker. If you need to know the details, then read what is SSL. For the same reason, if a website asks you about your things such as your banking details, then, first of all, do not forget to check whether it is a secure URL or not. And such a website should use some security protocol in its URL so that the consumer's information is not misused. I advise you to take special care of all these things before giving any personal information. I think by now you must have understood how important a sitemap is, if you want that there is no miss of any page of your website, then you have to take care that those crawlers do not miss any page.

You can also add additional metadata such as change frequency and priority. Along with this, you can also create a sitemap for video and images. And once you've created the sitemap, don't forget to validate it and notify the search engines.

CHAPTER SEVENTEEN

What is DigiLocker?

The Modi government launched the Digital India Revolution in India during its tenure from 2014-2022. This revolution had digitized many government schemes and payments. Along with money transactions, many such online companies came into existence which used to give you facilities like booking, recharge sitting at home. One of them is Digilocker, where today we will talk about what this digilocker is and how to use it. This app was launched to save documents safely online. It's been almost five years since it was launched, but most people still don't know about it. That is why today I will give you detailed information about this app. You will get complete information on when, where and how to use it.

What is Digilocker?

A digital locker or digilocker is a kind of virtual locker that was launched by Prime Minister Narendra Modi in July 2022. This is an important part of the ambitious programme of the Government of India. Through this, users can keep important documents like birth certificate, passport, educational certificates, etc. safe online. To get this facility, the user must have an Aadhaar card authorized by the Government of India. If you understand in easy language, the way you keep your jewellery etc. safe in the locker of the bank. In the same way, the digital locker is also a way to keep your documents safe. The only difference is that here you save your documents online. That is, you can also call it an online safe to protect your important documents. You all know how important documents are in today's time. If you lose a document by mistake, then you may have to face many difficulties. For this, it is necessary that you keep them. We have many documents like PAN Card, voter ID Card, Passport, driving license, birth certificate, and income tax returns which we often need. We carry these documents manually which is a bit difficult as well as unsafe. In such a situation, it is necessary that these documents should be kept in one place so that in an emergency, your family can also easily access these documents. It is not possible to keep documents manually, so it is necessary to be paperless. However, for this, you can use free cloud storage like Google Drive and Dropbox. But both of them are operated by the US (foreign company). That is why they do not get any direct security under the IT Act. Keeping these things in mind, the Indian government launched Digilocker to provide a personal cloud storage service. Digilocker is your personal online document storage facility provided by the Government of India. Every applicant of the digital locker scheme gets a personal storage space of 10MB linked to an aadhar. Where e-documents and URI links can be kept safely. You can also e-sign all these papers, which is similar to the process of self-attestation.

How safe is Digilocker?

Talking about the security of Digi Locker, it is as secure as our bank account or net banking. For security, even in Digi locker, we have to create a user ID and password. After that we have to link it to our Aadhaar card. We also have to register our mobile number. Only after doing all these processes can you create your account in digi locker. So much security is not even available in any bank's website, net banking, this means that it is much safer than the bank's net service.

What can you keep in DigiLocker?

You should also know what documents you can keep in your G-Locker. So that you can use it properly.

You can keep the following documents in digi locker,

- Driving Licence
- Registration Certificate
- Pollution Certificate
- Voter Id-Card
- Pan Card
- Income Tax Return
- Property Tax Receipt
- Marksheet of school, college
- School, College Certificates
- Registry of houses, land
- Important private, government documents

Let's now know how this digital locker can be used.

How to use Digital Locker?

You'll need a few guidelines to use Digilocker. To keep all your papers safe on this, you have to create your account on its website or app.

Let me tell you about it in step-by-step detail.

How to create an account on DigiLocker?

There are 2 ways to create an account in Digilocker.

- With Aadhaar card
- Without an Aadhaar card

The first one is easy, so let's talk about that first.

1. Aadhaar Card Moethd

- You can sign-up in DigiLocker from the Aadhaar card number.
- DigiLocker is available on the Google Play Store. That's why you can install this app from here.
- Sign-up after opening the app.
- Enter your mobile number after that. You will receive an OTP. Submit the OTP and set your user name and password.
- After creating a DigiLocker account, you can also sync the DigiLocker account from Facebook or Gmail.
- You can scan and upload proof of your educational documents and identity/address here.

This was the way to sign-up through the app on Digilocker. You can use this method on the website as well.

2. Non-Aadhaar Method

- In this method, you can sign-up by authenticating your mobile number and then manually uploading your identity and address proof.
- After creating an account on Digitlocker, you can upload your personal documents to it, let's also know about it.
-

How to upload documents to Digilocker?

When you have created your account on DigiLocker, you will have to click on the upload documents option to upload the papers. Note: Each file to be uploaded should not exceed 1MB.

- Select the Upload Documents option.
- Then press the Upload button.
- Now choose the location of your document.
- Then select the file and click on the Open button.
- Click on select Doc Type for any document in the Upload Documents list.
- Select the document type from the drop-down list and click on Save.

Note: Keep in mind that the format of the files in your documents should be in Jpeg, PDF, Jpg, Png and Bmp formats.

E-Sign Document/Certificate: For each document uploaded, the uploaded documents section contains an e-sign link. After clicking on it you will receive an OTP. After entering this OTP, click on the E-Sign button.

Let me tell you another important thing only one document can be e-signed at a time.

How to share documents?

If you want to share your e-documents, then you get the share link in the section of uploaded documents. After clicking on it you will be asked to enter the e-mail. Type the e-mail of the person you want to share your papers with and click on the send button. You can only share one document at a time.

What are the benefits of Digilocker?

You must have known this from the information given above, yet let us tell you according to its benefit points here.

- You can access it anywhere and at any time in the world.
- You get a guarantee of security here. That is, your papers are completely safe.

- Copies of original documents and certificates can now be kept digitally and some certificates like driving license, registration certificate, and mark sheets do not need to be copied anymore. Because signed copies can be obtained from the source, making them verified record copies of the certificate.
- Having a verified record allows you to find your college or school marksheet directly in your digi account.

Suppose you have studied at a college, your marksheet can be released directly in your digiLocker.

- Documents in DigiLocker can never be damaged.
- There will be no fear of losing after saving papers here.
- You will not have to carry documents with you in the interview all the time. You can even give your company a link to the paper so that your document will be checked easily.

There are many more such advantages, which are provided to us by Digi Locker, by using it we can keep our documents safe. It is a great thing that our documents are safe on the government website and not on a third-party website.

Friends, we told about the important scheme of the Government which is really one of the biggest needs of today's era. We learned what Digilocker is and how it is used.

Also, in this chapter, I have told you about the safety and benefits of digital lockers. I hope that you have now got full knowledge of it and you will use it as well.

CHAPTER EIGHTEEN

WHAT IS BITCOIN?

What is Bitcoin? Bitcoin is a digital currency that acts completely free of charge, that is, no bank or government has control over it. A completely virtual currency. You can also understand the online version of the cache. Since Bitcoin is decentralized digital cash, a peer-to-peer computer network is used to complete all its transactions, i.e. all purchases here are made by confirmed users. At the same time, there is no bank or government here at all.

Nowadays, it has become possible to earn money with the help of the internet. There are so many ways in which we can earn money from the internet while sitting at home. One of those ways is Bitcoin, because of which we can make a lot of money. Some of you may have heard about Bitcoin and those who do not know anything about Bitcoin will find out through this article today. Yes, today I am going to tell you about what Bitcoin is.

What is Bitcoin?

Bitcoin is a decentralized currency, which means it is not tied to a specific country or currency. It is a currency built on top of blockchain technology, which means that transactions made with Bitcoin are publicly and chronologically stored on the blockchain. This means that one can see all the transactions made so far.

Bitcoin was introduced in 2009 by an individual or group under the name Satoshi Nakamoto. Bitcoin meant a way of creating a digital version of cash, where payments could be made from one person to another without having to pay through a financial institution or another middleman who could charge for this type of payment and slow down the processing time. Anyone can use Bitcoin like we all use the internet and it has no owner, just like bitcoin.

Why is Bitcoin used?

We can use Bitcoin to make online payments or to make any kind of transaction. Bitcoin is considered to be the fastest and most efficient to use in transactions. Nowadays, many people are adopting Bitcoin such as online developers, entrepreneurs, non-profit organizations, etc. and because of this, bitcoin is being used for global payment all over the world.

As we make online transactions using the rest of the currencies, then we have to follow the payment process of the banks, only then we can make the payment and the account of every transaction we have made be present in our bank account so that it can be found out where and how much money has been spent, But no one owns Bitcoin, so the transactions with it are recorded in a public ledger (account) which is called bitcoin "blockchain". All the transactions made with Bitcoin there are details stored and the same blockchain is proof that the transaction has taken place or not.

Bitcoin Today's Rate

The value of Bitcoin today is about $16,456, which means that the value of a Bitcoin is Rs. 13,65,000. Its value is more or less because there is no authority to control it, so its value varies according to its demand.

What is Bitcoin Wallet?

We can only store bitcoin electronically and we need a bitcoin wallet to keep it. There are many types of Bitcoin wallets such as desktop wallets, mobile wallets, and online/ online wallets. Using a web-based wallet, hardware wallet, and one of these wallets, we have to create an account in it. This wallet gives us a unique ID as an address, such as suppose you have earned bitcoin from somewhere and you have to store it in your account, then you will need that address there and with the help of that you can keep bitcoin in your wallet.

Apart from that, if you have to buy or sell a bitcoin, then you need a bitcoin wallet and after that, whatever money you get in exchange for the bitcoin that you sell, you can also transfer it to your bank account through a bitcoin wallet.

How to Earn Bitcoin?

Bitcoin can be earned in three ways. Here is the complete information on how we created a Bitcoin account.

The first way is that if you have money, you can buy a bitcoin directly for $999. It's also not that if you have to buy a bitcoin, you have to pay $999 in all. Just like in India, there is 100 paise in 1 rupee, in the same way, 1 bitcoin has

10 crore satoshi, then you can buy the smallest amount of bitcoin satoshi and deposit 1 or more bitcoin slowly. When you have bitcoin and its price increases, then you can make more money by selling it.

The second way is that if you are selling a product to someone online and if that buyer has bitcoin, then you take bitcoin in exchange for money from him, in such a way that you will also sell them the goods and you will also get bitcoin which will be stored in your bitcoin wallet. If you want, you can also get a profit later by selling that bitcoin to the sheer at a higher price.

The third way is bitcoin mining. For this, we will need a computer with a high-speed processor whose hardware should also be good. We use bitcoin only to make online payments and when someone makes a payment with bitcoin, that transaction is verified.

Those who verify these are called miners and those miners have high-performance computers and GPUs and they verify the transactions through them. They verify whether the transactions are correct or not or if there is any manipulation in them. In return for this verification, they get some bitcoins as a reward and in this way, new bitcoins come into the market. Anyone can do this, it requires a computer with a high-speed processor, which is not in everyone's budget to buy.

Just like in every country, there is a limit to printing the currency in a year that you can print only so many notes in a year, so there are some limitations with bitcoin in the same way that more than 21 million bitcoins cannot come into the market. That is, the limit of bitcoin is only 21 million, and more bitcoins will never be found. Talking about now, about 13 million bitcoins have come into the market and the new bitcoins that are there will now come through mining.

Benefits of Bitcoin

Now let's know what the benefits of Bitcoin are.

- Here your transaction fee is much lower than paying with a credit card and debit card.
- You can send Bitcoin anywhere and anytime in the world without any hassle.

There is no bitcoin account block here, as sometimes the bank blocks our credit or debit card for some reason, so that problem is not here.

- If you want to invest in bitcoin for the long term, then you can benefit a lot from it because it has been seen in the record that the price of bitcoin is increasing, then going forward, you may get a lot of profit from it.
- In the transaction process of Bitcoin, if any government or authority does not keep an eye on you, then many people use it to do the wrong thing, and then it is beneficial for them.

Disadvantages of Bitcoin

Now let's know what the disadvantages of Bitcoin are.

- There is no authority, bank or government to control bitcoin, so due to this, there are a lot of fluctuations in the price of bitcoin, and then it becomes a little risky.
- If your account is ever hacked, you will lose all your bitcoins and they can't even be brought back.

How to buy Bitcoin?

You can buy bitcoin as soon as gold, that too in Indian currency. So let's know that there are websites in India from which we can buy Bitcoin very easily, that too in our currency.

Here on these websites, you can easily see their price, that too in real-time. If you need information on how to buy Bitcoin in the past, read here.

1. Wazirx
2. Unocoin
3. Zebpay

CHAPTER NINETEEN

What is Plagiarism?

In today's time, it has become much easier to convey your knowledge and thoughts to people. There used to be a time when we had to resort to books to convey our ideas and knowledge to people. But today, we can easily reach out to people with the help of a blog or website online. In this chapter, we will learn what plagiarism is. We will also learn how we can find out about it as well as how to stop it.

Being online, it is quite easy that the information we have written can be copied very easily and republished in a blog. So, the content written in this way that is stolen is called plagiarised content. It is very important to stop this kind of theft because by doing so, one's hard work goes in vain and also causes a lot of damage to him.

What is Plagiarism?

When content available on a blog or website such as information, photos, videos, etc. is copied and used on another blog or website, which in a way we can call theft is called plagiarism. It can also speak of a kind of online theft or copyright. The person who wrote it is the one who owns it. And it is illegal to use the content created by him in another place without his will. Against which action can also be taken. Such theft can be detected. There are so many tools online that can help you find out if anyone is stealing your content. There are so many useful tools available that allow you to do this work.

Now let's understand it easily. Let's say you've written a poem. It's your words. After a lot of hard work and spending a lot of time, he threaded these words into sentences and then wrote them down in one place. Now with the work you have done, you hope that it will reach out to people and they will like it, which also benefits you financially and also gives satisfaction that someone got to learn that the words you have written will make someone happy. But when someone copies his poem without your knowledge and writes it to another website, you will not be happy to know this at all. On the one hand, you will be angry and would like no one to use your words anywhere without your consent. That's what we call Plagiarism. Now you must have understood what it is and what difference it makes.

The pitfalls of plagiarism?

- It's a job that doesn't do any good but only causes harm.
- The work you do is stolen which causes a loss of your royalties.
- When you write some information very hard and reach out to people which benefits them and in return, you earn some money. When someone else copies the same information on their website, then the people who come

to your website or blog start going to it too. Which causes you a lot of damage.

- When your blog ranks on Google, there is good traffic on it, but when your content is copied to another website, Google gets confused about who is the original. Unless you know that your content is copied and don't tell Google that you are the original owner of that content, Google won't even take action on it. So, your ranking can also fall and your traffic can also go.
- Those who do wrong things like Plagiarism, whether intentionally or unknowingly, do wrong things in a way and should know that they can be fined for it. Apart from this, the blogs are doing good work so they may have to face copyright too.

Whenever you write any information on your blog, after writing it, make sure that it is not available from a website or blog. For this, you can use it which will let you check a line to tell if it is copied from somewhere or not. Because if you publish such information contained on your website or blog, it will never rank. Because wherever you are copying, all of its data is already available with Google and it will not be too late to know where the content you put inside you was picked up.

How do you know plagiarism?

If you're writing or have written content and want to know if you don't get it right from somewhere, you're not. So, for this, you can now use many online tools that will tell you in a very accurate way whether your content is getting along with the chain or not. I've already used a lot of online tools to check my content and I'm giving you information about milk them that works for me and I know it works well. It's quite easy to know if your content is plagiarised or not and can be easily detected. For this, you just have to copy your content, take it to that website and just paste it and submit it. Which will find your content line by line and search to tell which line of yours is plagiarised.

CHAPTER TWENTY

WHAT IS CYBER SECURITY?

Cyber Security Kya Hai - Friends, you have to know what is Cyber Security, its definition, how it works, and what are its types. If you know, you may not know everything, then after reading this you will know the full information.

What is Cyber Security?

Cyber security is a type of security that is a security for systems connected to the Internet. Through this, the data of hardware and software is made even more secure so that data is not stolen in any way and all documents and files are protected. Cyber security is made up of two words cyber + security, meaning whatever is related to the internet, information, technology, computer, network, application or data, we call cyber. While security is related to security, which includes system security, network security, application and information security.

How Does Cyber Security Work?

Under Cyber Security, there is a large team of ethical hackers who protect your data from being stolen, data deleted or any of your devices damaged. Those who work in cyber security prevent bad people from doing the wrong thing. Under this, your network, computer system, program and your data are kept secure.

Why is cyber security important?

- Cyber security is essential to protect our data such as images, PDFs, text documents or any other type of data that resides on our computers.
- Cyber security is very important to keep any data that contains only our copyright safe. For example, if you have a company, it is necessary to have only your copyright on its data, so that no one steals it or someone else can use it.
- Cyber security is also very important to protect our banking and financial data because if our banking data is not safe then any hacker can withdraw money from our bank account.
- And nowadays, internet banking has become an essential part of life, so it is important to keep banking and financial data safe.
- Cyber security is also very important for national security. National security means that nowadays there are cyber-attacks on the defence system of our country.
- There are also some data or information that are very necessary and sensitive, such as nowadays, even in government offices, most of the work is done through the internet.

- If the data of a government office is leaked, then it can also cause a lot of damage. Therefore, cyber security is also very important to keep this type of data safe.

Types of Cyber Crime:

- **Hacking**: In this type of cybercrime, hackers enter the restricted area and access another person's data and sensitive information, without the permission of that person, the restricted area can be someone's personal computer (PC), mobile or an online bank account (Net Banking).
- **Cyber theft:** In this type of cybercrime, the hacker violates copyright law, it is a part of cybercrime which means theft committed through a computer or the internet. This includes identity theft, password theft, information theft, theft of internet time, etc.
- **Cyber Stalking:** This cybercrime is more visible on social media sites. In this, stalkers harass and harass a person by repeatedly sending dirty messages or emails. In this, stalkers often make small children and people who do not know much about the internet. After this, stalkers start blackmailing that person, this makes the person's life very difficult.
- **Identity Theft:** This type of cybercrime is seen a lot nowadays. In this, hackers target people who use online cash transactions and banking services such as Google Pay, Phonepe, and Paytm. Hackers somehow get a person's data such as account number, debit card details, internet banking details, etc. information and withdraw all his money, due to which that person has to face a lot

of financial loss.

- **Malicious software:** If a lot of such dangerous software is created by a hacker, then you can not only steal the data of the computer or mobile connected to any internet but also delete it, as well as with the help of this software hackers can crash your entire system. There are many types of software such as malware, spyware, viruses, ransomware and worms. Hackers send this type of software mostly to another computer via a link, pop-up message, or email and ask to touch the link seductively. If that person touches the link, then the entire control of the computer goes into the hands of the hacker.
- **Phishing:** In this type of cyber threat, the hacker sends a message or email to a person as a trusted entity or bank, which looks quite valid when seen. The purpose of the hacker behind this is to take sensitive information of the person such as bank account number, debit card, Aadhaar card, etc. and cause him financial loss.
- **Child Pornography and Abuse**: In this type of cybercrime, hackers mostly use chat rooms and talk with courtesy by hiding their identities. Young children or minor people do not know much and gradually hackers interrupt children for child pornography. Apart from this, children are not able to tell anything to their parents due to fear.
- **Man in the Middle (MITM) Attack:** In this type of cybercrime, the attacker who is the attacker keeps spying on the communication of two people and after some time, one of those two people becomes one of the two people, and the information needed from the front, and sensitive data such as a bank, debit, credit card details, etc. This does not even let the person in front of

him know and the hacker gets all the information.

- **Denial of Services (DoS):** The main purpose of the DoS attack is to reduce the traffic of a network or website. In this attack, hackers suddenly bring too much traffic to a network or website and weaken the network system. Along with this, there are many services like email, yahoo, Hotmail, etc. In these, when there will be a lot of traffic suddenly if any user goes to log in, then the user will not be able to use that service.
- **Spoofing:** In this type of cyber-attack, the hacker can attack the system of a large server or a large company using the identity of another human being. By resorting to this attack, a hacker can ruin someone's life.
- **Salami Slicing Attack:** "Salami Slicing Attack" is also known as "Salami Cheating". In such a cybercrime, the cyber-criminal carries out a big attack by making a lot of small attacks. Attackers deduct a very small amount of money using customer information such as bank/ debit card details. Due to the small amount of money cut, customers are unaware of slicing and do not even complain about it, which does not detect the hacker. It is only a strategy to benefit from small increments from time to time.

Apart from these, there are many more cyber-attacks, with time, new types of these are also being detected.

Types of Cyber Security:

In cyber security, the user is provided with different security in different layers of the network. All the crimes mentioned above are committed online and the 6 best cyber security to prevent them are as follows:

1. **Network & Gateway Security** – This can be called the first layer of the network. You must have heard the name of the firewall on the computer. It is a wall for a network that allows only safe things to enter and keeps out unsafe threats.

1. **Data Loss Prevention (DLP)** – In this process, all the data of the user is fully encoded, using SSL (Secure Sockets Layer). Under this protection, information or data is encrypted to keep it away from Unauthorized Access.

3. **Application Security** – The applications being used by it in the network are followed by a security process. So that the shortcomings of that application can be removed. Also, if the application is unsafe, it is removed from the network.

4. **Email Security** – If you use Gmail, you may have noticed that some emails go to the Spam folder. This happens because spam filters are installed in the network for email security. So harmful emails can be kept out of the reach of the user because most crimes are committed through email phishing.

5. **Antivirus Security** – Everyone has antivirus on their computer. It protects our computers from different types of viruses. After all, all our sensitive information and private files are stored in the computer itself, so it is very important to keep it safe.

6. **Network Access Control** – It is used to keep unauthorized users and devices out of the network. NAC

protects the functionality of the network, ensuring that it has access to only authorized users and devices. Network operators decide which devices or applications comply with endpoint security requirements and whether they will be allowed network access.

Advantages of Cyber Security

- With the help of this, we can be protected from unauthorized access so that there is no risk of any kind of data loss.
- With the help of Cyber Security, we can keep our network secure so that we can use the Internet.
- Your personal and sensitive data is provided with a security cover so that hackers do not exploit you financially or mentally.
- Information security is better and business management also increases.
- Online cash transactions are quite popular nowadays, so you can make secure transactions with cyber security.

9 798887 726694

Printed by Libri Plureos GmbH in Hamburg,
Germany